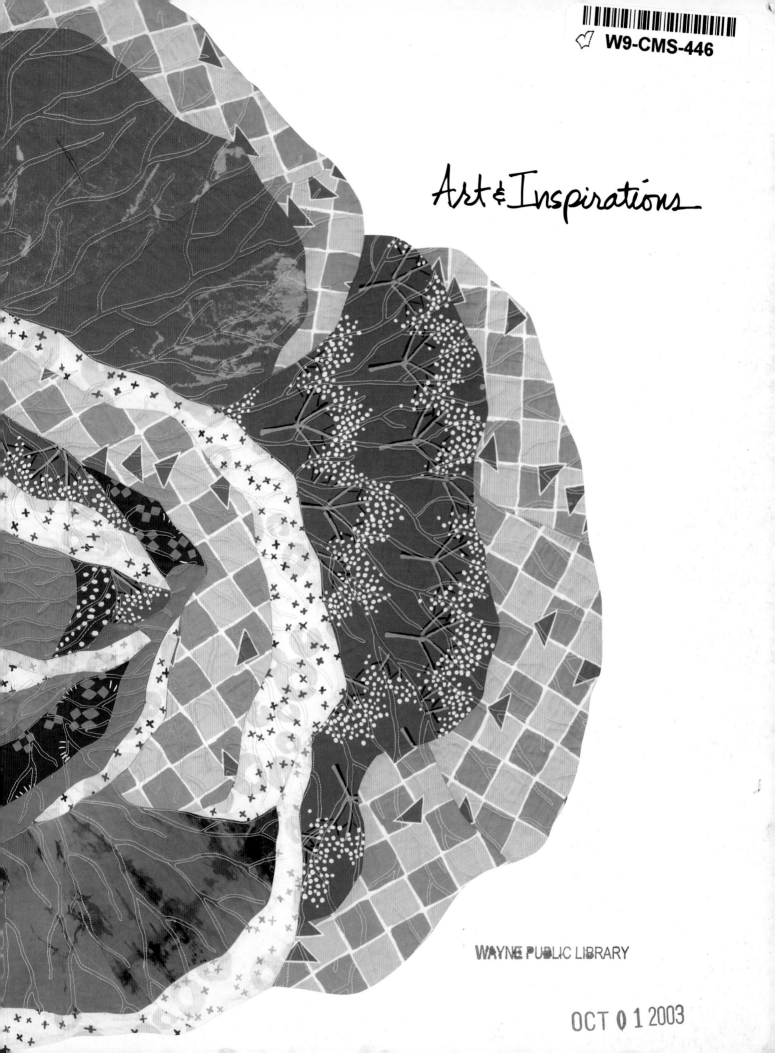

Art & Inspirations

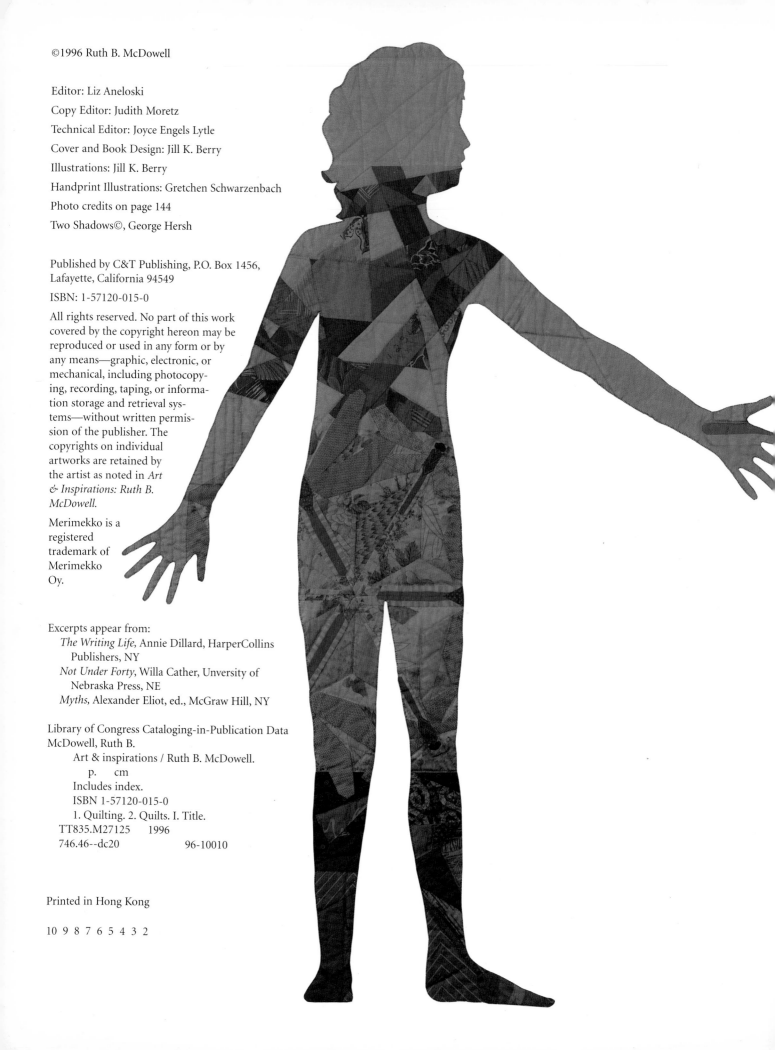

©1996 Ruth B. McDowell

Editor: Liz Aneloski

Copy Editor: Judith Moretz

Technical Editor: Joyce Engels Lytle

Cover and Book Design: Jill K. Berry

Illustrations: Jill K. Berry

Handprint Illustrations: Gretchen Schwarzenbach

Photo credits on page 144

Two Shadows©, George Hersh

Published by C&T Publishing, P.O. Box 1456, Lafayette, California 94549

ISBN: 1-57120-015-0

Excerpts appear from:
The Writing Life, Annie Dillard, HarperCollins Publishers, NY
Not Under Forty, Willa Cather, Unversity of Nebraska Press, NE
Myths, Alexander Eliot, ed., McGraw Hill, NY

Library of Congress Cataloging-in-Publication Data
McDowell, Ruth B.
    Art & inspirations / Ruth B. McDowell.
        p.   cm
    Includes index.
    ISBN 1-57120-015-0
    1. Quilting. 2. Quilts. I. Title.
TT835.M27125   1996
746.46--dc20   96-10010

Printed in Hong Kong

10 9 8 7 6 5 4 3 2

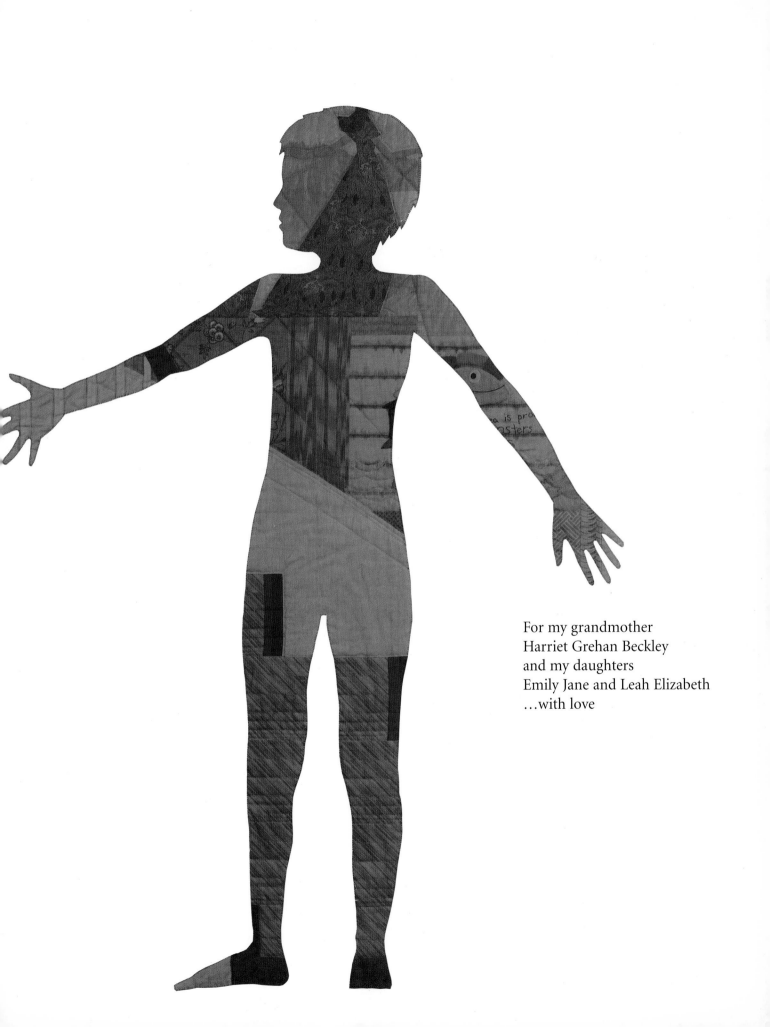

For my grandmother
Harriet Grehan Beckley
and my daughters
Emily Jane and Leah Elizabeth
...with love

Table of Contents

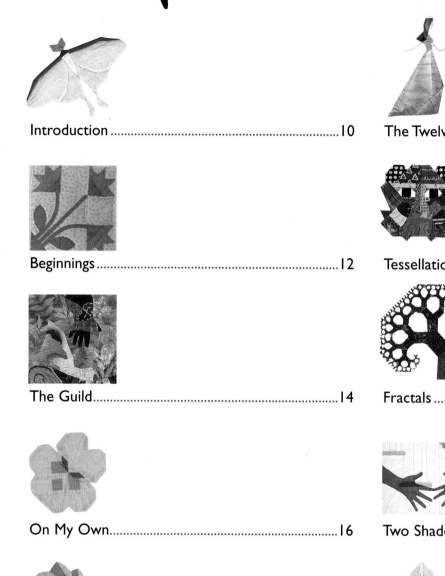

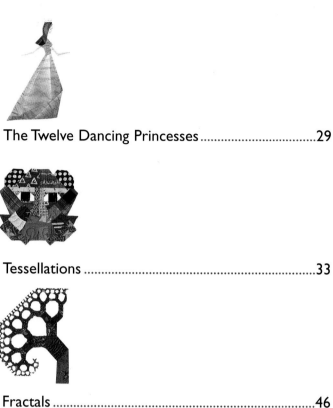

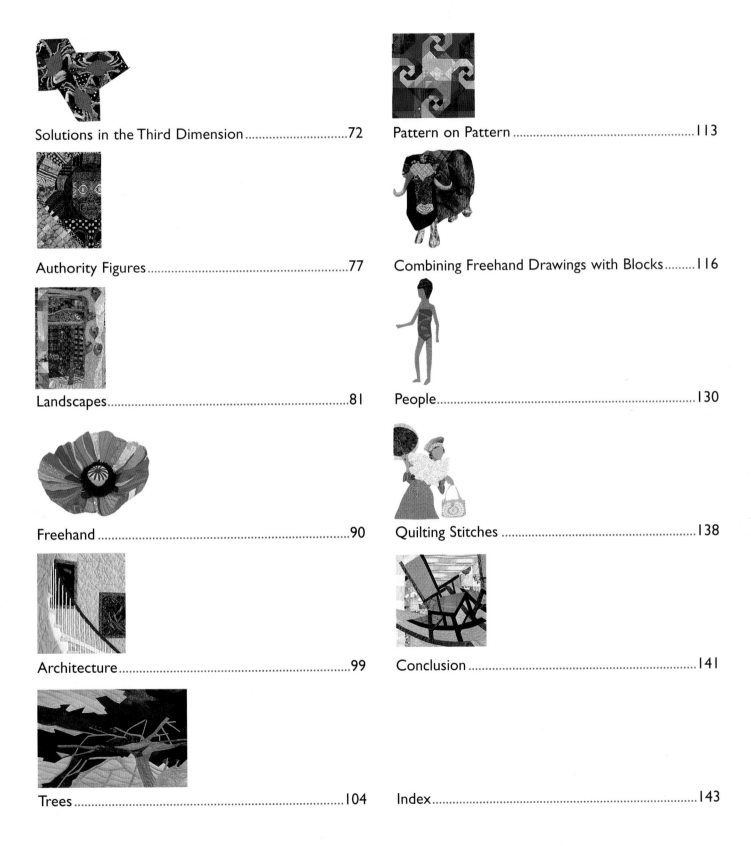

Introduction

"*Women derive a pleasure, incomprehensible to the other sex, from the delicate toil of the needle.*"

Nathaniel Hawthorne
The Scarlet Letter
1837

The only reasonable way to write this book seems to be to begin at the beginning and go on to where I am now. As I continue with this process of making quilts, interests change, themes weave in and out, ideas percolate for a while, then suddenly burst to the surface when the time seems right.

My best quilts happen through a process that is certainly non-verbal, and usually not logical in any commonly accepted sense of the word. But a conjunction of things seen/heard/felt with fabrics/patterns/images starts a conversation that is recorded in a quilt.

My academic background in the field of fine arts is certainly not the usual one. Aside from abstract Form and Color, and Light and Color courses from an architectural curriculum, I missed studio art and art history almost entirely, graduating from MIT a year before my degree, B.S. in Art and Design in the area of Visual Design was officially offered.

This has had consequences, of course, in my work. I have spent a fair amount of time reinventing the wheel, discovering things most fine arts majors were taught early on. On the other hand, I never learned what I was not supposed to do, or what was politically incorrect in the established art world. This has had the liberating effect of allowing me to escape the embarrassment I should apparently sometimes be feeling.

I wish I had taken more drawing and art history classes before and during college. In pursuing this quiltmaking career full time for fifteen years, I have gradually learned some of this on my own.

You will not find pictures of my studio or living space in this book. My interest is the quilts. A lovely spacious studio and a magazine-style home have, of necessity and by choice, been a very low priority for me. Suffice it to say that my spaces are continually right on the border of chaos.

In choosing a label for myself, I have become comfortable with calling myself an artist. This is not to try to set myself up as part of an elite group. We are all artists in some way when we try to do the best we can, whatever our field of creative endeavor. Using your gift to express yourself in a way that forms a strong connection with others is the common thread.

A Word About These Quilts

The great many traditional patterns quiltmakers have used over time have been handed down as common property, as part of the heritage of quilts, to be borrowed, copied, adapted, or used as each individual saw fit. In presenting the material in this book I have shared with you my thoughts and ideas, methods of working, construction tips, quiltmaking philosophy, and images of many of the quilts I have made over the past twenty-five years for your amusement and inspiration.

All of my quilts are copyrighted. The quilts from my previous books, *Pattern on Pattern*, The Quilt Digest Press, 1991 (*Maple Leaf, Monkey Wrench,* and *Double T*) and *Symmetry: A Design System for Quiltmakers,* C&T Publishing, 1994 (*Painted Daisies* and *Bull Frogs*) were made available as patterns to the quiltmakers of the world with the publication of those how-to books. I hope my quilts will encourage you to explore your own vision as an artist and quiltmaker and suggest many paths to pursue in developing your own designs.

Please do not copy the quilts presented here, but adapt the ideas to make your art your own. As a professional artist, I retain the copyright to all of this material. Please respect my work and my rights as I respect yours.

Noon Day Lily
96" x 67", ©1972
machine pieced, hand appliquéd, hand quilted,
blends, polyester batting (artist's collection)

Beginnings

I've always been fascinated with making things—tea sets from acorns, functioning bow and arrows from flat toothpicks, doll clothes made with scraps of fabric, and collecting or salvaging useful and beautiful bits and pieces, then sometimes using them in a new way.

Using my hands and eyes in exploring colors and textures led to a gradual interest in sewing (the variety of fabrics!), knitting (oh, the colors of the yarns!), crochet (easy to invent your own little pieces), needlepoint and counted cross stitch (fun to design on graph paper). My education in art came only in college, in the Architecture Department at MIT. It certainly didn't approach things from the same angle as most schools of fine arts. Design in architecture was challenging, the drawings and models were fun, as was playing with color, proportion, value and line, but it was not the right time or place psychologically for me to become an architect.

After a brief career as a technical illustrator, my husband and I bought an old house. I turned my attention to gardens and plants, wallpapering, painting, and continuing my interest in fibers. To use up sewing scraps I made a couple of quilts using four-inch squares, having a great time arranging the disparate collection in the process.

Interest in quilting had been growing rapidly throughout the country with the approaching 1976 Bicentennial. Quilt books were becoming more widely available. In 1972 I found Ruby McKim's book, *101 Patchwork Patterns*. The style of her text was delightful. Her original blocks based on poppy, iris, rose, and trumpet vine were graphically interesting, botanically recognizable, and straightforward to piece with traditional methods. The trumpet vine, being a rather unusual plant to choose, especially attracted me.

Inspired, I decided to make a pair of matching Noon Day Lily twin-size quilts. I invented a border combining the pieced flower block with hand appliquéd stems and leaves. The local fabric stores were filled with polycotton blends, the new miracle fiber combination. I found white and orange fabrics (these were to be day lilies, *hemerocallis*), and a tiny calico print. A no-iron sheet from Sears was a better green than those available in the fabric stores. I was too inexperienced to recognize that hand appliquéing pieces of a percale sheet was going to be traumatic. (Percale sheet threads are packed so tightly together that it is very difficult to stick a needle into them, a point worth considering when embarking on hand appliqué.)

At this point I usually have to stop and remind people who are new to quilting that rotary cutting hadn't been invented in 1972. Making a pair of matching twin-size quilts in the old-fashioned method meant tracing around the orange petal diamond template 408 times with a pencil, then cutting each petal out individually with scissors. It could take a week to cut out a quilt. The idea of buying yardage so you could cut it into pieces and then sew it back together, which sometimes seems absurd, was even more so in 1972.

Since I was experienced with a sewing machine, machine piecing was a logical choice and an enjoyable process. I persevered and produced two tops.

This preference for machine piecing has continued. It was reinforced by the fact that my hands sweat all the time. With hand piecing or hand appliqué, the needles corrode and stick because of the dampness. Machine work minimizes that problem.

Since no one who saw my quilts knew anything about quilting either, everyone was greatly complimentary. I got a full-size quilting frame, and proceeded to teach myself to hand quilt with stitches that were relatively even and about one-fourth of an inch long. I entered one of the quilts in a quilt show at the Woodlawn Plantation in Virginia and went with a friend to Washington to see the exhibit. Seeing the quality of the construction on the other quilts made me aware that I still had some way to go.

The Guild

A few years later I stumbled on a quilt show five miles from home. The Quilters Connection guild in Arlington, Massachusetts, was a few years old, and in their annual show at the First Parish Church hung work from *all* of their members, from beginners to the likes of Nancy Halpern, Rhoda Cohen, and Michael James. What an eye opener!

The Quilters Connection guild, a group covering the whole spectrum of approaches to this medium, insisted from the beginning that their annual show would be open to all members, with no jurying of entries and no prizes awarded. The diversity of the group would be its strength. A varying group of guild members, including Nancy and Rhoda, have hung each year's show with intelligence and sensitivity, in a single intense day. There were no categories of contemporary quilts and traditional quilts, bed quilts and wall quilts. All the quilts were hung together, complimenting and contrasting the individual styles, and awarding to each the same degree of respect.

Drawing the pattern for *Swimmers*©

That philosophy continues to this day, and I hope for the rest of the life of the guild. The concept that this is a community, not a competition, gives everyone a chance to grow. We are all richer for the experience.

As I travel to teach at other guilds around the world, each seems to have developed its own personality. Many of my students have shifted from one guild to another until they find a group they are comfortable with. Some belong to several guilds. Some students seem stifled or intimidated in some quilt guilds. Others thrive on the challenge of competitions and scoring systems. It is important to begin to recognize where you fit into the myriad of possibilities available in the study of quilts and quilting.

The local tradition of the quiltmaking/needlework community in a particular area has had an impact on the contemporary scene. Where there have been strong continuous county and state fair traditions, with ribbons and prizes, that practice has often been carried over into judging and prizes in present-day quilting events. Other guilds, arising from an informal grouping of friends, have become less involved in rules and competitions. Some of the patchwork schools in Japan seem to be organized in a traditional Japanese pattern, focused on a head teacher.

Within a quilt guild or group there will be a great variety of interests: traditional quilts, contemporary art, history, textile study, writing, design, crafting, and community service projects. Ranking one avenue over another devalues us all. The breadth of the quilting community is our strength. Let us recognize and respect our diversity.

That first quilt show experience put me in touch with the developing quilt world. There were a few local stores which carried fabrics and notions especially for quilters. I found that wonderful solid colors in cotton fabrics were available by mail from Cabin Fever Calicoes. *Quilter's Newsletter Magazine* gave me a glimpse of what people were doing with quilting in other parts of the country. And there was a growing body of quilters in my neighborhood that shared this new found passion of mine.

Nancy, Rhoda, and Michael had been working creatively in quilts for some time and each had begun to develop their own distinctive style. Michael used mostly solids, precisely piecing strips and curves. Nancy employed a wider range of fabrics and made lyrical geometrical quilts, usually on natural themes. Rhoda had a much freer style in choosing fabrics and construction, appliquéing, reverse appliquéing, hand piecing, or even machine piecing as she chose.

With the possibilities quiltmaking offered to make my own statement, I found a medium that felt just right to me for the first time.

I cannot express the debt I owe to Nancy and Rhoda. As we got to know each other, they opened my eyes in numerous ways. Their great friendship and wildly divergent styles of quiltmaking made it easy for me to make the necessary choices to begin developing a personal style of my own.

Complaints that "too many quilters call themselves artists" arise now and then. For me, this is a false issue. *Time* will determine which quilts are significant as art.

Meanwhile, the body of work and the process of growth we each undergo should be the focus of our energies.

Since 1981 I have been part of a small group including Nancy Halpern, Rhoda Cohen, and Sylvia Einstein, and various other people at various times. We've tried to keep the size to six or seven, meeting roughly once a month. Over a pot of coffee we talk about what we've seen and where we've been since the last time, trading books, catalogs, and extra fabrics.

Over the years we have become more comfortable with each other.

We each usually bring something of our present projects to talk over with the others, to get help or suggestions for possible changes or admiration, or to explore new trains of thought.

Much more than the larger guild, this group has been extremely valuable to me. Although the four of us have been together for so long, we each have quite disparate styles and methods of working, which don't seem to have gotten appreciably closer over the years. I especially value having an opportunity to see my work through other eyes, and to begin understanding these different points of view.

Swimmers
57" x 81", ©1994
Rhoda Cohen, Sylvia Einstein, Beatriz Grayson, Nancy Halpern, Ruth McDowell, machine and hand pieced, hand appliquéd, machine quilted, cottons, blends, cotton batting (artists' collection)

On My Own

Over the next few years, while caring for my daughters Emily (b. 1976) and Leah (b. 1978), I tried different approaches, looking for the part of quilting that felt like my own. Full-size *Wild Goose Chase* and *Lone Star* quilts, made of cotton, machine pieced and hand quilted, improved my technical skills and gave some room for creativity as well. My *Lone Star* has an unusual rolling half-star border. Still being a technocrat, I figured the length of the border by adding a long string of mathematical calculations using the square root of two. Surprisingly, my addition was correct and the border fit.

Two Celtic Interlace-inspired pieced quilts let me play with some of the wonderful shades of solid cottons available by mail. I designed a twelve-inch Nasturtium block in the style of Ruby McKim and made a careful colored pencil drawing for a Nasturtium wallhanging. At the fabric store I ran into a problem finding the sky-blue

Wild Goose Chase
92" x 78", ©1977
machine pieced, hand quilted, cottons, polyester batting (artist's collection)

and nasturtium-leaf green of the colored pencil sketch; neither color was available that year from the fabric companies. Changing my color scheme entirely to work with the material available, I learned my lesson about designing in color. In every quilt since then, the color choices were made only with the fabrics themselves.

These early quilts were primarily made of solid colored fabrics because they looked very graphic and modern. As I continue to work, my fabric selections have expanded, urged onward by Nancy, Rhoda, and Sylvia. Prints, plaids, batiks, ikats, dress and furnishing fabrics, and rummage sale finds give me the opportunity to greatly vary the visual surface with pattern, texture, scale, and even historical references.

For me, quiltmaking is a salvage medium, using available materials, as has been the quiltmaking of the past. Although there is a much wider choice

*Y*ou adapt yourself, Paul Klee said, to the contents of the paint box. Adapting yourself to the contents of the paint box, he said, is more important than nature and its study. The Painter, in other words, does not fit the paint to the world. He most certainly does not fit the world to himself. He fits himself to the paint.*

*Annie Dillard,
The Writing Life, 1989*

in fabric available today, quiltmakers are still limited unless they choose to dye, paint, or otherwise manufacture their own fabric. Limits are not always obstacles, however. Limits can force new ways of looking and working creatively.

I prefer to work with found materials, including hand dyed fabric from some of the excellent hand dyers, because it interests me to work with the medium and against these limits.

Naturally, sometimes I have less of one fabric than I think I need. I'm convinced if you run out of a fabric and have to find something else to use in your design, it's always a more interesting quilt in the end.

Lone Star
105" x 90", ©1978
machine pieced, hand quilted, cottons, polyester batting (artist's collection)

Nasturtium
64" x 53½", ©1980
machine pieced, hand appliquéd, hand quilted, cottons, polyester batting (private collection)

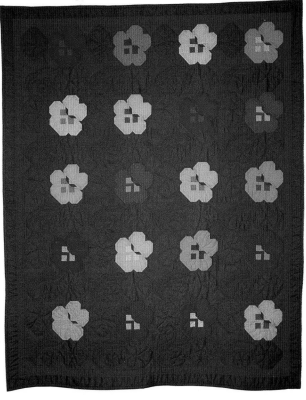

Herb Quilts

The Quilters Connection guild has offered workshops to its members since its founding. Two were especially significant to me in getting started: Masterpiece Scrap Quilt, taught by Rhoda and Nancy, and Strip Piecing by Nancy Crow. Masterpiece Scrap Quilt was full of exciting exercises in working with color in fabric, demonstrating the advantages of choosing fabrics for quiltmaking from a different point of view than you would for clothing and the variety of possibilities for design within the simple traditional block format. A lecture by Nancy Crow, with her dramatic quilts and positive, energetic approach to quiltmaking, followed by a workshop in strip piecing, gave me a push to develop my own style.

The day after the strip piecing workshop I took a pad of graph paper into my garden to see what was there. Since it was early spring in New England not much was up, but there was a clump of celandine pushing through beside the fence.

Celandine
40" x 40", ©1980
machine pieced, hand appliquéd, hand quilted, cottons, polyester batting (private collection)

To most people celandine is a weed, but it has a long and interesting history as a medicinal and dye plant. As a gardener in a former life, I had spent considerable time learning about herbs and their history from the fascinating members of The Herb Society of America. All of that information resonates whenever I see one of those familiar plants.

Celandine is a member of the poppy family. It has very pretty leaves, three-quarter-inch yellow flowers, and fork-like seed pods. The juice in the stems is brilliant orange. Growing in a rosette, the plant suggested it might work as a central-medallion style quilt.

From those observations, and using Nancy Crow's strip piecing with dramatic darks in the background, I developed a sketch for a forty-inch square *Celandine* quilt. The quilt was machine pieced, with a single yellow flower hand appliquéd in the center. When it was finished I felt certain this was the beginning of what I was meant to do.

There followed a series of forty-inch square quilts based on familiar plants and herbs: *Borage II, Lady's Mantle, Angelica I, Sweet Woodruff, Foxgloves I* and *Bee Balm I.*

Above: Borage II
40" x 40", ©1981
machine pieced, hand appliquéd, hand quilted, cottons and blends, polyester batting (private collection)

Below: Angelica I
40" x 40", ©1980
machine pieced, hand appliquéd, hand quilted, cottons, polyester batting (private collection)

Above left: *Foxgloves I*
40" x 40", ©1980
machine pieced, hand quilted, cottons, polyester
batting (private collection)

Above right: *Sweet Woodruff*
40" x 40", ©1981
machine pieced, hand appliquéd, hand quilted, cottons,
polyester batting (private collection)

Left: *Lady's Mantle*
40" x 40", ©1981
machine pieced, hand appliquéd, hand quilted, cottons,
polyester batting (private collection)

Opposite page, top: *Bee Balm I*
40" x 40", ©1980
machine pieced, hand quilted, cottons, polyester
batting (private collection)

Opposite page, bottom: Bee Balm

Bee Balm, *Monarda didyma*, is an American native, a member of the mint family. It has square stems and simple opposite pairs of leaves. Its flower heads are formed of thirty or forty florets and do not, at first glance, seem to be a likely subject for pieced quilt design. The design of *Bee Balm I*, a radical simplification of the flower itself, was a significant learning experience in abstraction to distill the essence of the plant. Eliminating most of the florets and focusing on a sunburst of six red check marks was enough to do the trick.

Machine piecing lots of little pieces does not bother me, as I had discovered in the traditional quilts I had made. *Bee Balm I* was cut from templates, pieced in the traditional way with straight seams (no Y seams), and made of the cottons and calicoes then available for quiltmakers.

With a great deal of trepidation I entered *Bee Balm I*, *Lady's Mantle*, and *Borage II* in Quilt National '81. When the reply letter came, accepting two of the three quilts, I was ecstatic. I called one of my sisters on the phone in great excitement, to tell her, "Nancy, Nancy, I'm going to be famous! They accepted two quilts in Quilt National!"

Emily, then four and a half, promptly collapsed onto the floor. "I'm nothing but a dreary old four-year-old," she wailed. "I'm going to throw myself onto the junk heap. You're going to be famous and I'm not!"

Now, Emily had been born talking as far as I can tell, and began reading before she was two, so this vocabulary was not out of the ordinary for her, but this was not exactly the response I expected.

Anyhow, it was delightful to hear congratulations from the quilters about this series, and it solidified my determination to make quilts.

Symmetry

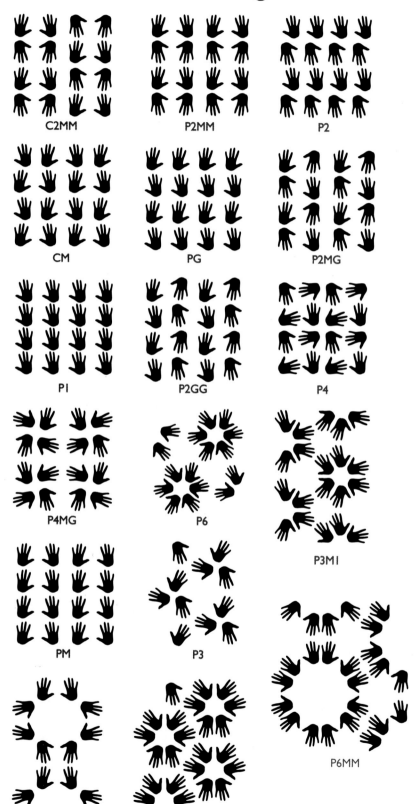

C2MM

P2MM

P2

CM

PG

P2MG

P1

P2GG

P4

P4MG

P6

P3M1

PM

P3

P6MM

P4MM

P31M

Earlier that spring I had exhibited four of my herb quilts at The Quilters Connection Annual Show. I was gallery-sitting late one evening when an older couple came through the exhibition. As the husband looked at each quilt, he wrote a note in the catalog. Expressing interest in my Herb Series, his wife asked if I had been to art school.

When I confessed that I'd graduated from MIT, her husband came over to ask why the quiltmakers at the show had used only four of the seventeen symmetries of a plane in their work. He suggested Martin Breuger's book on crystallography.

I was mystified, but found the crystallography book, which lead into a whole other area of quilt design, my Symmetry Workshop, and eventually to my own book, *Symmetry, A Design System for Quiltmakers*.

Making a series of seventeen small quilts to help myself understand the system, I set about developing a method to explain this to quilters. Many quiltmakers have never had a successful math experience, although they may be very quick at visual patterning; others are math or science majors. In any one workshop I have all types, and all levels, the uniting factor being their interest in quilt design.

I often recommended Peter Steven's elegant book, *A Handbook of Regular Patterns: An Introduction to Symmetry in Two Dimensions*, which contains the design information, with many examples. Many of the less mathematical students had difficulty using Steven's patterns in quiltmaking.

Talking with my hands seemed to be a direct approach, so I chose to describe the symmetry patterns with handprints. The position of the hand relates to the position of the quilt block.

Handprint descriptions of symmetry patterns

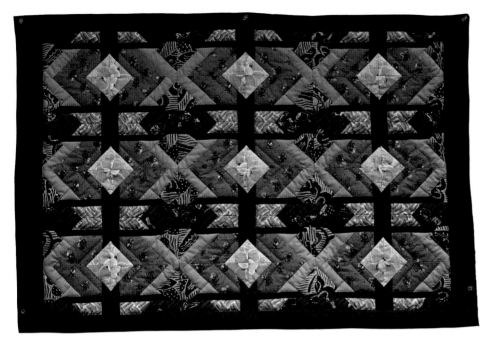

P2MM

Left: *P2MM*
28" x 39", ©1982
machine pieced, hand quilted by Carol
Marrochello, cottons, polyester batting
(private collection)

Below: *CM*
24" x 52", ©1982
machine pieced, hand quilted, cottons,
polyester batting (private collection)

Since most quiltmakers are familiar with the concept of a repeated geometric quilt block, I began symmetry with the students using a simple asymmetric square block design. Relating the symmetry studies to traditional quilt blocks gave me a chance to introduce the concept of symmetry vs. asymmetry, and to look at traditional blocks in a new way.

As a teacher of design, I try to begin in such a simple way that every student can participate and not feel intimidated. Too many students think they have no skills.

Breaking the process down to the point where students can let chance help to make the original design, if they want to, can be useful. Then showing them the extraordinary variety of patterns they can make with symmetry concepts builds confidence to the point where they can really get started with design. As the students become more familiar with the process, new possibilities can be suggested that can be followed to make more new designs. The key is to help everybody to begin.

CM

A more complicated symmetry quilt from 1982 is *Aquatic Rabbits*, inspired by the work of M.C. Escher, who used both symmetry and tessellations in his paintings and drawings. For *Aquatic Rabbits* I set out to plan a quilt in P6 symmetry, with equilateral triangular blocks, which would contain no background. Each piece that wasn't part of a rabbit would form part of a fish.

A design of this kind is fraught with compromises: move a line to improve the shape of the rabbit, and you've simultaneously distorted the carefully designed fish. Then add to that the technical problem of producing a block that can physically be pieced.

Anyone under the age of twelve usually picks out the rabbits and fish right away. Most older people have more difficulty, which is interesting in itself.

The rabbits are made from no-wale corduroy, with the nap of each piece running from the rabbit's nose to its tail. Since the rabbits are seen turned in all directions, they appear to be different shades of brown.

The quilt was hand quilted by Carol Marrochello. Her sons, then nine and twelve, were greatly concerned that the rabbits didn't have tails, so, when we finished the quilt, we sewed pompons to the back wherever there should have been a rabbit tail.

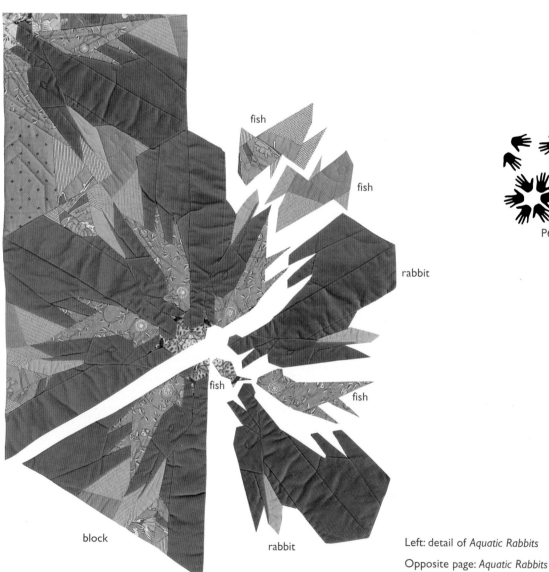

fish

fish

rabbit

fish

fish

block

rabbit

P6

Left: detail of *Aquatic Rabbits*

Opposite page: *Aquatic Rabbits*
117" × 94", ©1982
machine pieced, hand quilted by Carol Marrochello, cottons, blends, no-wale corduroy, polyester batting (artist's collection)

P4

Painted Daisies
69" × 69", ©1992
machine pieced, hand quilted by Carol Marrochello,
cottons, cotton batting (artist's collection)

After many years of presenting this concept of symmetry designing as a workshop, I wrote a book, *Symmetry, A Design System for Quiltmakers*, C&T Publishing, 1994. It included not only the handprint system of notation, but seventeen new quilts as well. The quilts were designed to take advantage of the particular characteristics of each of the symmetries. Templates, instructions, and yardage charts are included for all the quilts.

Painted Daisies uses P4, a four-way pinwheel often found in traditional quilt blocks. Here the initial block is a rectangle, which results in the necessary addition of small blue squares to complete the quilt.

Taking advantage of the mirror line on one edge of a right triangular block in P4MM symmetry, I made the pattern for *Bull Frogs*.

Bull Frogs
66" x 66", ©1992
machine pieced, machine and hand quilted, cottons, cotton batting (artist's collection)

P4MM

The traditional pattern Double Wedding Rings is awkward to piece by machine. This design, for a six-inch square block, goes together easily in P4MG symmetry and can be adapted in many ways.

Above: *Spinning Rings*
72" x 72", ©1992
machine pieced, machine quilted, cottons, cotton batting (artist's collection)

Left: detail of *Spinning Rings*

P4MG

The Twelve Dancing Princesses

On the Friday before Memorial Day, 1982, Emily and Leah went to their grandparents' house for a weekend in the country. They were six and four and had never been away from me overnight. My marriage was falling apart, and I needed some space to regroup.

Suddenly, with no babies in the house, the peace was amazing. I could think consecutive thoughts, use the bathroom without being interrupted, and set my own schedule for meals. What freedom!

One of my favorite stories as a child had been the tale from the Brothers Grimm of *The Twelve Dancing Princesses*, or *The Shoes that Danced Themselves to Pieces*. The multiple images in the story; twelve princesses, three groves of trees, twelve princes in rowboats, seemed perfect for the repeated blocks in a patchwork quilt.

My sewing room at the time was on the third floor, with a maximum ceiling height of six feet four inches, sloping down from there to the eaves. There was no vertical wall on which to pin up work in progress. Happily working away in the quiet, I designed the piecing for a princess, a nearly-invisible soldier, and a formal grove of trees. When the kids came back on Monday night, I was ready to begin sewing.

The Twelve Dancing Princesses or *The Shoes that Danced Themselves to Pieces*
140" x 102", ©1983
machine pieced, hand quilted, cottons, blends, satin, brocade, beads, polyester batting (Ropes & Gray collection, Boston, Massachusetts)

The Twelve Dancing Princesses

Once upon a time there was a king who had twelve beautiful daughters. Each night he locked them in their bedroom. Each morning when he let them out, their dancing slippers were full of holes. The king couldn't figure out how his daughters got out of their room to dance each night away, so he promised that any man who could solve the mystery would inherit the kingdom and the hand of whichever daughter he fancied.

Many princes came to try their luck, but the princesses would drug them with wine, and the princes would sleep through the ensuing frolics. Finally a poor soldier appeared who had acquired a secret invisible cloak from an old crone in the forest. He pretended to drink and fall asleep.

The princesses promptly rose, dressed, put on their dancing shoes, and followed the eldest down a secret staircase that unfolded from her bed. Wrapped in the invisible cloak, the soldier followed after them, snapping off a leaf from the grove of silver trees, the grove of golden trees, and the grove of diamond trees through which they passed. On the shore of a lake twelve princes waited in twelve rowboats. Slipping into one boat with the youngest princess, the invisible soldier was rowed to a magnificent castle where everyone danced all night.

Well, the soldier had such a great time, he followed the princesses for three nights before he told the king. Then, since he was not as young as he used to be, he chose the wise eldest princess for his wife and they lived happily ever after.

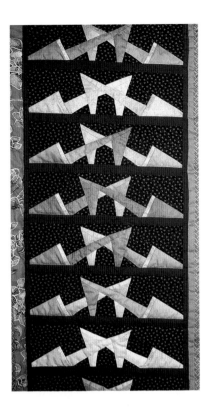

Opposite page: detail of the Invisible Soldier

Top left: detail of the Dancing Slippers

Top right: detail of the Gold Grove

Above left: detail of the Boats and Princes

Right: detail of the Castle

After piecing the three center panels, I began a design for the border which was to include twelve pairs of slippers, princes in rowboats, a castle with fireworks, the secret staircase, and the princesses' row of beds.

detail of the Beds

While I was describing this with great excitement to Nancy Halpern on the phone one day, she stopped me with another idea. She said, "Remember that quilt by Bertha Stenge, called *The Quilt Show*, with each of the sixteen blocks showing a colonial lady holding up a different miniature patchwork quilt?" Unfortunately, I knew which quilt she was referring to. "You'll have to make patchwork quilts for those beds," said Nancy. So the top border of the quilt contains the Nancy Halpern Memorial Seminole-Pieced Bed Quilts in one-point perspective.

I was having so much fun with the story, I never stopped to figure out what the total dimensions of the quilt would be. When I tried to spread the top out on the living room floor so I could see what it really looked like, it didn't fit. A quilt 102-inches wide and nearly 140-inches high is a rather large size for a wallhanging.

The top was finished to bring to our September Show and Tell guild meeting. Almost everyone liked it.

After I finished the hand quilting in January 1983, the quilt was shown at a few exhibits, then sold that fall to one of the big Boston law firms as part of their corporate art collection.

That sale, and several other smaller ones, led me to the naive conviction that this career I'd embarked on might actually work financially. My husband and I were divorced in November 1982, and I had to find some way to earn a living for me and my children.

In addition to providing an income from teaching and the sale of quilts, becoming a professional quiltmaker would enable me to work at home and set my own work schedule, fitting the quilting in between nursery school car pools and all the parenting that two lively children require.

Sympathetic older women told me that having to balance this complicated set of demands would pay off in unexpected ways in the end. Maybe that is so.

As I have found, setting up as a professional artist is a chancy living. My kids, having grown up in this household, have gotten a realistic view of what's involved in such a choice.

Tessellations

People had by this time begun sending me articles from *Scientific American* and other journals in the mail in plain brown wrappers. One wonderful article from *Scientific American*, July 1975, titled "On Tessellating the Plane with Convex Polygon Tiles", p.112-117, dealt with the geometric shapes that could be used for tessellations. This clearly had applications to quilts.

We knew squares, rectangles, right or equilateral triangles, and regular hexagons tessellate (tessellate: fit together with themselves to cover a flat surface with no holes and no overlaps). We had seen Postage Stamp, Brickwork, Thousand Pyramid, and Grandmother's Flower Garden quilts, but apparently plenty of other shapes for quilt blocks or quilt patches could be used as well.

For instance, any triangle will tessellate.

Any quadrilateral (four-sided) shape will tessellate. You can pick the oddest four-sided shape you'd like, no sides parallel, no sides equal length, and it will fit together with itself to cover a quilt top. The edges of the quilt top may be irregular with an irregular quadrilateral, but that problem can be dealt with in other ways.

I had many, many more block shapes to play with than the traditional square. As I made more quilts exploring unusual tessellations, the reaction from quilt experts would sometimes be, "Ruth McDowell hasn't strayed far from the traditional in her quilts." Very few viewers would notice that a quilt might be composed of "tessellating irregular complex pentagons of Type seven," for instance, but a few mathematicians and engineers began to take notice.

Transformations 1
53" x 88", ©1982
machine pieced, hand appliquéd, hand quilted, cottons, blends, polyester batting (private collection)

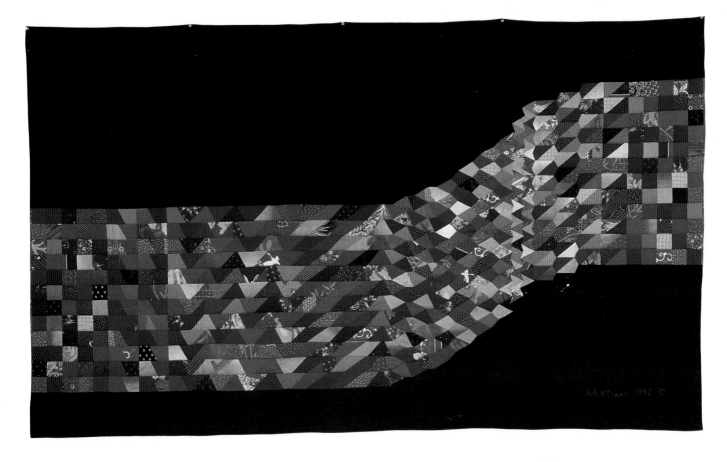

The Toaster Incident

About this time I was invited to give my first lecture to a guild in which I had to fly to the meeting (from Boston to Syracuse, a flight of an hour or so). My sister Marilyn, who lived in Syracuse with her family, offered to come to stay at my house in Winchester and care for my kids while I was away. What a deal! We decided I would spend the night at her house in Syracuse between one lecture and the next.

My first slide lecture went well. Among the quilts I showed were a few with tessellations, and I mentioned casually that since any triangle or quadrilateral would tessellate, these shapes could be possibilities for quilt blocks.

After a very busy day, I arrived at Marilyn's house ready for a light snack and an early bedtime. Since she was away for a week, she had carefully cleaned out the refrigerator. There was some cold beer left, and bread and butter in the freezer. Toast and beer seemed just right after my elegant luncheon with the guild, so I popped the bread in her toaster and found the bottle opener.

Her toaster was the regular old-fashioned kind with slots in the top and a button that said "Push." The toast didn't pop up very soon, so I peeked in the toaster to find the bread getting darker and darker. I pushed "Push." Nothing happened. Frantic that my supper was burning, I picked up the toaster, turned it upside down, and dumped out the toast.

Forty years of crumbs promptly fell into the electrical wires and burst into flames. Time has a habit of slowing down, I find, in emergency situations. I watched as the six-inch flames licked her kitchen curtains. Pulling the toaster away from the window, I plunked a handy iron frying pan on top of it to smother the fire. The flames came out around the frying pan.

Then the light dawned. "Pull the plug!" The flames died down in the unplugged toaster. The toast was now cold, so the frozen butter wouldn't spread. So I grabbed my cold dry toast and my beer bottle, jumped in her king-size bed, and turned on the TV.

A short time later the phone rang. It was Marilyn checking to see how things were. I explained the near disaster, and inquired, by the way, how she managed to turn off the toaster when she used it.

"That toaster," said Marilyn, "was a gift from our mother. She got it at the church rummage sale. You just keep your eye on it and when the toast looks about right, pull the plug."

After another beer it was nearly nine o'clock, and I was very sleepy. The phone rang again. When I answered, it was a lady who had been to the lecture that morning. "You said," she informed me irately, "that any quadrilateral will tessellate. I went home and cut out a hundred of the same irregular quadrilaterals and they don't fit together at all!"

There was a long pause. Never, in my wildest dreams had I ever contemplated having to explain how to do this over the phone. But then the answer came in one of those rare flashes that you congratulate yourself for years afterwards. "You put sides of the same length together. With identical irregular quadrilaterals (or triangles), match the side lengths by twisting the quadrilaterals around, but not flipping them over. Works like a charm."

Mentioning irregular quadrilaterals leads of course to irregular quadrilateral quilts. The Primrose quilt began with a large irregular quadrilateral block within which I pieced a group of primrose leaves.

Primrose flowers are composed of five symmetrical petals. I designed and pieced many primrose flowers with regular pentagonal blocks, then joined flowers of the same color together in irregular clusters.

Because I find it a more comfortable way to work, and because I like the flat surface of a totally pieced quilt, I cut holes in the pieced blocks of leaves and inserted (pieced in) the flower clusters by machine.

The background fabric resembled a tablecloth, so I used a traditional blue and white tablecloth as the backing fabric, making sure it was exactly on grain, as were the pieced fabrics in the top. By stitching a narrow zigzag about 1½ inches from the edge through all layers, and removing the batting outside the stitching, I could then fringe the top and backing of the quilt to produce this edge.

This seemed like a useful way to pass the time on a long plane flight to the west coast, though a bit startling to an adjacent passenger in a pin-striped suit.

Top: Primrose blocks

Right: *Primroses*
44" x 42", ©1985
machine pieced, hand quilted, cottons, blends, polyester batting
(private collection)

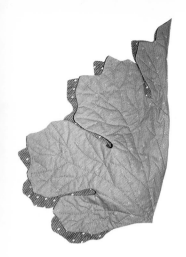

The receipt of a very generous commission from the New England Quilters guild to make a quilt for their new museum's collection was a chance to use some very unusual geometry again.

My focus was on New England flora. I had also become interested in two-sided and three-dimensional quilts. The quilt I constructed represented the small wildflower bloodroot as it emerged from its protective leaf wrap in response to the early spring sunshine. Some of the petals and some of the leaves are three-dimensional quilted insertions. The back of the quilt was pieced as a much more abstract design.

The leaves representing the forest floor are pieced from a single geometric shape, a very particular irregular convex pentagon. Drawing this "tile" was complicated and required some careful thought.

The loose leaves were sewn using two green fabrics, right sides together, seamed along the outer edges with a layer of thin batting. The seam was trimmed, clipped, and the leaf turned right side out. After hand quilting the vein pattern on the leaf flap, the raw edge of the leaf flap was inserted in a seam of the pieced top.

The loose petals were prepared in a similar manner, but with a heavy interfacing in place of the batting.

After piecing the top and the back, I assembled the quilt sandwich on a large table, feeling through the layers to make sure the sweeping curves of the top and the back were aligned before pinning them together. The piece was then hand quilted and finished with a separate casing at the top for hanging purposes.

For another tessellation, see Delphinium block on page 73 in Solutions in the Third Dimension.

Below: *Bloodroot*
70" x 114" x 7", ©1986
machine pieced, hand appliquéd, hand quilted, two-sided, insertions, cottons, blends, silks, interfacing, polyester batting (New England Quilt Museum, Lowell, Massachusetts)

Above: detail of *Bloodroot*
Below: back of *Bloodroot*

Penrose and other Non-periodic Tiling

Among the *Scientific American* articles were several dealing with some very unusual tiling systems. The ones that attracted the most notice were those of Roger Penrose.

In my tessellated quilts so far, there had been an underlying grid in the ways the tiles repeated that was still quite prominent. With non-periodic tiling systems like Penrose's, many of the tessellations looked much more disorderly, almost as though they were crazy quilt patterns, but made with simple repeating units.

Over a series of years I have worked with non-periodic tilings in a number of quilts and explored the possibilities for quilt design with many workshop students.

Robinson Tiles

Historically, one of the earlier non-periodic tiling systems that was developed is called Robinson Tiles. One set frequently illustrated uses a series of six tiles in which the corners and edges have been deformed in very particular ways. As an illustration for a workshop, I made my own versions of the six Robinson Tiles: one set pieced baskets, one set pieced faces, and several geometric designs.

At the urging of some students I blithely set out to piece the Robinson Tile faces. The quilt I designed was made of forty blocks, each twelve inches squarish. In fact, each edge of each block was made up of at least five angles. This is not a tiling system recommended to everyone as a source of pieced quilt design.

Below and opposite page: Mr. Robinson blocks

Opposite page, top: *Mr. Robinson*
105" x 116", ©1991
machine pieced, hand quilted, cottons, blends,
polyester batting (artist's collection)

In *Penroses* I have exploited the five-fold symmetry of a Penrose sun to make wild roses, a five-part flower.

Left: Detail of *Penroses*

Below: *Penroses*
59½" x 48", ©1984
machine pieced, hand appliquéd, hand quilted, cottons, blends, polyester batting (private collection)

The flowers of the five-petaled geraniums are made of a smaller set of Penrose Kites and Darts, a reduction of the kite and dart set that composes the body of the quilt. In this case I have chosen an area of kite-and-dart tiling in which the radial symmetry is not so apparent. The zoned geranium leaves are pieced in the larger size kites.

Geraniums
76½" × 65", ©1984
machine pieced, hand quilted, cottons, blends, polyester batting (artist's collection)

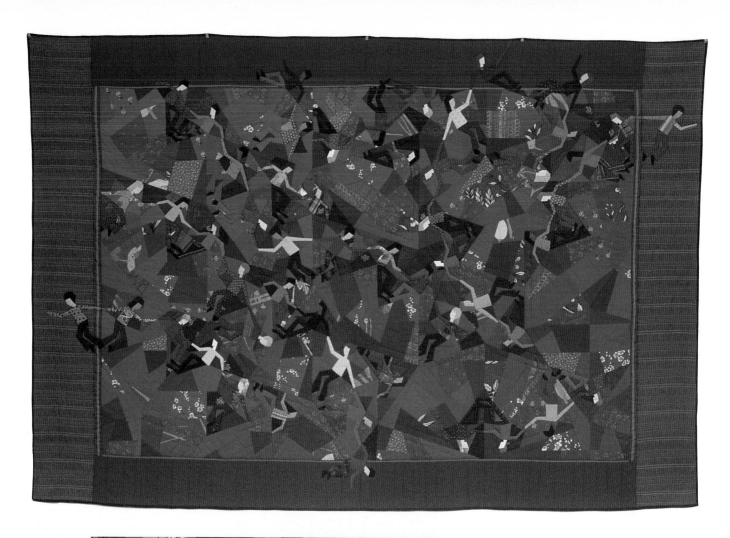

In *Cherry People Pie,* piecing children into Penrose Kites and Darts with their hands in particular places makes short chains of figures dashing in different directions. Studying the pattern carefully today, I can find a mistake in the kite-and-dart tiling in this quilt, but rare is the viewer who points it out.

Top: *Cherry People Pie*
55" x 81", ©1984
machine pieced, hand quilted, cottons, blends, polyester batting (private collection)

Left and above: detail of *Cherry People Pie*

Above: white pine

Right: *White Pines*
74¹/₂" x 52", ©1988
machine pieced, hand appliquéd, hand quilted, cottons,
blends, polyester batting (private collection)

Below: detail of *White Pines*

Driving around the countryside with
these tiling systems on the brain, I was
struck by the needle clusters of Eastern
White Pines. Here, in *White Pine*, the
kites and darts make a foreground tree
on the right side of a forest landscape.

Fractals

Over the years I have collected articles in the field of fractal geometry. Looking at the illustrations of fractals from a visual point of view, it seems as though a geometric pattern is set up, then repeated over and over in a regular way, using a constantly increasing or decreasing scale.

In thinking of fractals in terms of traditional quilt blocks, I noticed that the Noon Day Lily flower has a right angle at the bottom of the base triangle, and additional right angles between the four diamond-shaped petals. You can draw progressively smaller lily blocks in a regular way, as is shown in *Fractal Lily*.

The smallest (fifth generation) lily blocks are drawn with machine quilting and accented with a few appliqués. The traditional set for *Noon Day Lily*, on page 12, is illustrated in the machine quilted background for the piece.

Fractal Lily
77" x 77", ©1990
machine pieced, hand appliquéd, machine quilted, cottons, blends, polyester batting (artist's collection)

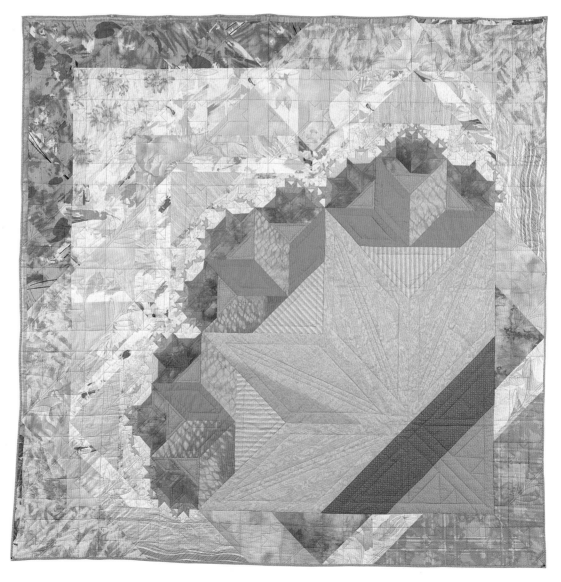

Above: *Baobab With Snail's Trail*
84" x 101", ©1994
machine pieced, hand appliquéd, machine quilted, cottons,
cotton batting (artist's collection)

Right: detail of *Baobab With Snail's Trail*

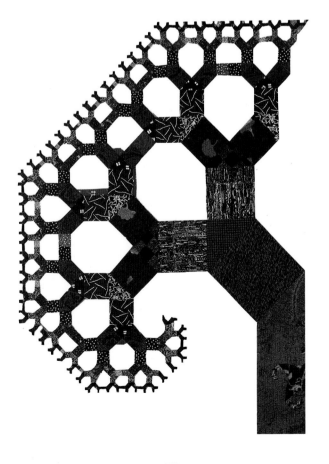

A much more recent quilt is *Baobab with Snail's Trail*. This comes from a classical fractal pattern called Pythagorean Tree which was introduced to me by Diana Venters of South Carolina. She is a math teacher as well as a quilter and, finding this pattern in a book, made a small appliquéd version. It seems quilt-like, because it is composed of squares and half-square triangles.

I was intrigued at the similarities I could see between the Pythagorean Tree and the traditional Snail's Trail block, and made a pieced quilt combining the two.

Recently many junior and senior high school teachers have become interested in the relationships between geometry, quiltmaking, visual design, and history. Moistening some dry geometry with all the color and design in quilts creates enthusiastic students.

Two Shadows

Two Shadows © by George Hersh

In 1985, while lecturing and teaching for East Bay Heritage Quilters in Berkeley, California, I was taken out to dinner by several of the members, including George and Diane Hersh. Diane was very actively involved in quilting and in EBHQ. George was becoming interested in quilting, after getting involved in needlework embroidery.

We had a lovely and lively meal, with the conversation ranging over all sorts of subjects. Both Hershes came to my lecture later that evening and to the Symmetry workshop the next day.

A week later, an envelope arrived in my mail with the following story from George Hersh.

Once, in the old days, in the farthest place away, in an old house with an herb garden and a corkscrew staircase, there lived a witch with her two young daughters, who both had the witch gift, but not yet the control. The mother was a thread witch and she could sew what she could see. One daughter was a word witch and she could say what she could see. One daughter was a time witch and she could see what she could see. (Most people mix up what they see with what they think they ought to see.)

The mother sewed and pieced; tiles and herbs and princesses and patterns. Her piecing was cleverer than cats and defter than deer. The word witch talked and her words picked up things and people and put them in their places, or at least in some places. The time witch thought about what she saw and her thoughts could run like a river to the sea of time and truth.

Now you might think that in such a household all would be peace and plenty. And sometimes it was. But it was not always so.

The witch who stitched was all grown up and her needle ran with her heart and mind. Her quilts had the power to warm your heart and make your thoughts sing, as well as keeping your toes warm in the cold. But, like all magic, some people could not see it.

Especially since there were no labels on the quilts saying "You ought to look at me." So some days were feast days and some days were fast days and almost every day was filled with long, long hours of working to make the magic do as it was told.

The two young daughters found it hard to wait to be as free as their mother. They wanted to have all of their power and knowledge right now. It is very hard to wait for power and harder still to work for knowledge. It is much easier to squabble with your sister about now than to work for yourself towards then.

Three witches under one roof can mean lots of grumbling and sparks and "It's your faults" bouncing from floor to ceiling. Once in a while the big old house was too small to hold all three unless they stayed far apart; one in the workroom, one on the third floor, and one roaming from room to room, looking for company and finding trouble.

One stormy afternoon the witch who stitched had a new idea, an idea too strong to let simmer. She could see in her mind's eye a wonderful pieced quilt just waiting to be made. In the idea quilt there were no tiles or patterns, but her own two daughters in the pride and strength of their youth. Into her workroom she galloped. Graph paper and rulers and cloth and thread rustled and rattled until their sounds crept all the way up the corkscrew staircase to the topmost floor of the old wooden house.

Each of the two daughters peeked in at the workroom door and each went off as fast as she could go, for their mother's eyes were shining with magic like wolves' eyes in winter snow.

The thread witch sketched and snipped and never noticed how quiet the house grew around her. She worked and she worked and the pieced quilt grew with its images of her daughters in the pride and strength of their youth. She stitched like a fire running through dry grass, like the wind when it's wanted on the other side of the world, like a sunbeam when a cloud gets out of its way. The cuttings and selvages piled deep around her. About three o'clock in the morning she placed the last piece and stitched the last stitch and sat back and said "There!"

Then she yawned and stretched like a sleepy cat and went off to bed through the silent house.

The next morning, when the sun came up, the thread witch got out of bed, still yawning a little. She hung the new quilt top where you could see it from the breakfast table and waited for her daughters to come downstairs and see their wonderful pictures worked in the cloth.

But nobody came down to breakfast.

The thread witch waited and then she frowned a worried frown and then she called and then she climbed around and around the corkscrew staircase to the top of the house. But nobody was in their beds.

The thread witch called until her voice rattled the plates all the way downstairs in the kitchen, but there was no one to answer. Suddenly, she understood! Down the stairs she ran, two at a time, round and round and down and down until she came to where the new quilt top was hanging.

There were the two pictures, the word witch daughter and the time witch daughter, colorful, beautiful, perfect, silent, and motionless. The house was so still you could hear the laundry settling. Her daughters had become caught in her work.

"Oh, no!" said the thread witch, "I worked too well and I worked too fast. My daughters are caught in the spell of my work and I can't think how I'll get them out. If I rip their seams I might hurt them and if I cut them out they'll unravel."

Inside the quilt, the word witch struggled and strained to find the word that would let her out. She knew so many words, but she couldn't say one for herself with her lips stitched in place.

The time witch thought and thought, but time moves very slowly for a person who has become one hundred percent cotton.

At last, the word witch stopped trying to talk to the outside and the time witch stopped trying to speed up the inside. The time witch put herself to speeding up her sister. The word witch spoke to her sister along a row of chain stitches.

"Take my hand," she said to her sister. They reached out and touched in the time inside the quilt. Together they stepped out and rounded up to be real again, standing hand-in-hand on the kitchen floor.

"Thank goodness!" said their mother. "Now, hurry up and eat your breakfasts or you will be late for school. Next time I'll work more slowly and try to get just my love for you in a quilt without tangling your two selves up in it."

The quilt top was hanging with two daughter-shaped holes in it.

"Piece in the two holes with black silk," said the time witch daughter. "Then we won't get caught again."

"Yes!" said the word witch daughter. "And you can call it 'Two Shadows' and sell it to the Boston Museum."

And that's what the stitch witch did.

Here's the quilt I made to go with the story.

Above: *Two Shadows*
64½" x 92½", ©1985
machine and hand pieced,
hand appliquéd, hand quilted,
cottons, blends, silk, tulle,
polyester batting (artist's
collection)

Far left: detail of Emily shadow

Left: detail of Leah shadow

Opposite page, bottom: detail
of hands

Putting Things Together

As I proceed, my quilts tend to be created by a gradual braiding together of many different facets. Having used a variety of irregular quadrilaterals in two transformation quilts, I began to investigate the possibilities of combining unusual block shapes with my nature studies.

Fitting a Block to a Sketch

With *Jack-in-the-Pulpit* I began with a large freehand sketch based on a photograph of the plant. Looking at the sketch, I realized that a rectangular block sized to fit around the sketch would leave a large open corner at the bottom left, and another blank space at the top right. Because of my study of tessellations, I realized I could draw an irregular block for *Jack-in-the-Pulpit* that would fit more closely around the sketch, and still tessellate.

The block I chose has six sides. Actually, it began as a rectangle from which I cut off one triangular corner. Adding that same triangle to the opposite side allowed me to draw a block that would tessellate in rows. It fit the sketch and solved the problem of the blank corners, and made a much more interesting quilt visually.

Jack-in-the-Pulpit taught me a number of other valuable lessons in quiltmaking. I had a piece of burgundy, green, and white striped fabric on the shelf I had found a few years before with the intention of using it as part of a Jack. The outside of a Jack cup is, in nature, a much paler stripe than the inside surface. Using the same striped fabric wrong-side up for the outside of the Jack made a perfect contrast.

Wrong sides are often paler, even frosty or foggy looking. Some look completely different from the right side, others almost the same. Jack-in-the-pulpits generally grow in shady swampy places, so I used dark fabrics for the background pieces. Randomly cutting up large scale drapery prints, as I did here, implies many other undefined plants growing in with this one. Solid or small scale printed fabric used in the background would tend to isolate the plant and separate it from its environment.

The blocks in *Jack-in-the-Pulpit* are arranged in three rows, the top and bottom ones facing to the left and the center row facing to the right. This back-and-forth movement is possible with this block because the top and bottom edges of the block are parallel. *Jack-in-the-Pulpit* is, therefore, an example of glide symmetry.

Introducing drapery and furnishing fabrics into my quilting gave me a much greater range in scale of printed pattern and a more subtle choice of colors. If the fabrics are washed first, before being put in the quilt, they will soften enough to enable them to be hand quilted.

The choice of fabrics in a quilt is another place where individual decisions must be made. If the goal of the quiltmaker is to take tiny, prize-winning quilting stitches, heavier fabrics must be eliminated. I needed a greater range of fabrics, so taught myself to quilt through many different weights with a consistent and, to me, acceptable hand quilting stitch.

The large scale background fabrics for *Jack-in-the-Pulpit* were cut into pieces without paying attention to which part of the print showed up in each piece. When the blocks had been sewn, the completed blocks were shuffled into an arrangement that pleased me.

An alternative approach might be to carefully plan a particular part of the printed design in each piece of the patchwork. In some quilts this is important or necessary to produce specific design ideas. Random cutting, on the other hand, produces some interesting surprises and often gives the quilt a more unstudied feeling.

Above: *Jack-in-the-Pulpit*
51" x 60½", ©1983
machine pieced, hand quilted, cottons, blends, polyester batting (private collection)

Right: detail of *Jack-in-the-Pulpit*

Below: sketch of Jack-in-the-Pulpit block construction.

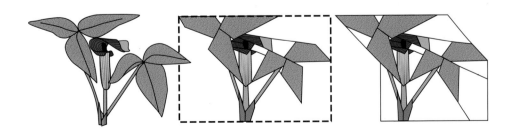

PG

Putting Things Together **53**

In *Mayapples* a single mayapple leaf is fitted into an elongated hexagonal block.

Above: *Mayapples*
39½" x 62", ©1986
machine pieced, hand quilted, cottons, blends, polyester batting (private collection)

Left: detail of *Mayapples*

Below: Mayapple leaves

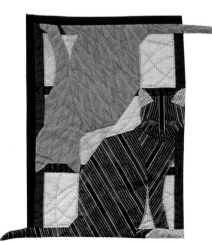

P2

After making a sketch, then figuring out a piecing diagram for a single cat for *Cat Tales*, I realized that two cats, one right side up and one upside down (P2 symmetry) would fit in a rectangle. In sketching the cat I focused on the face. There are two pieces in the cat's body and about eighteen pieces in the face. In laying out the quilt I realized that if I made the upside-down cats looking out the window, I would only have to piece nine eighteen-piece cat faces. This conveniently makes a more interesting quilt. The ends of the tails are loose, faced, and stuffed.

Above: *Cat Tales*
58½" x 45", ©1987
machine pieced, hand quilted,
cottons, cotton velveteen, blends,
polyester batting
(private collection)

Right: detail of *Cat Tales*

Fitting the Sketch to the Block

Using the kite-shaped block I had developed for P31M symmetry with its mirror lines, I designed a block for *Dragonflies*. One half of a large blue dragonfly was drawn on one long edge of the block. One half of a small red dragonfly was fit into the other long edge. All of the seams were straight, with two Y-seam intersections. When the blocks were assembled in the symmetry pattern, with reversed or mirror-image blocks, twenty-one red and twenty-one blue dragonflies took flight.

I included a piece of black tulle netting while I was piecing the dragonfly wings. It was simple to do and added veining to the dragonfly wings.

P31M

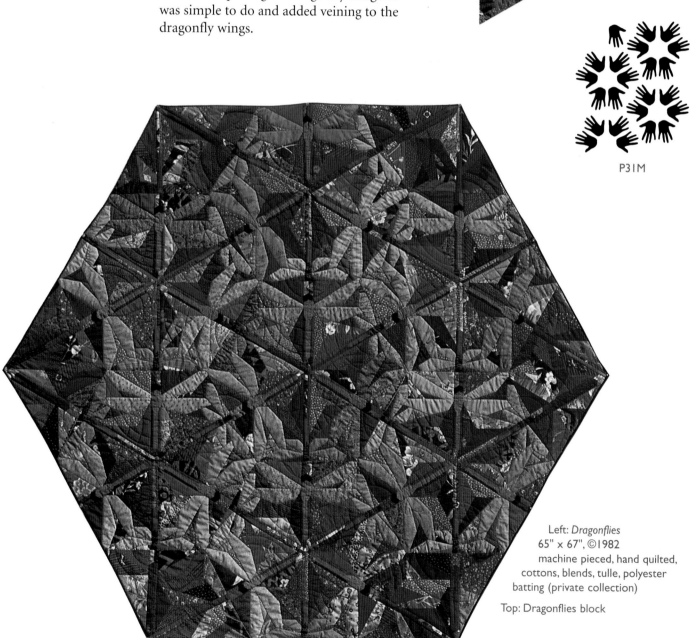

Left: *Dragonflies*
65" x 67", ©1982
machine pieced, hand quilted,
cottons, blends, tulle, polyester
batting (private collection)

Top: Dragonflies block

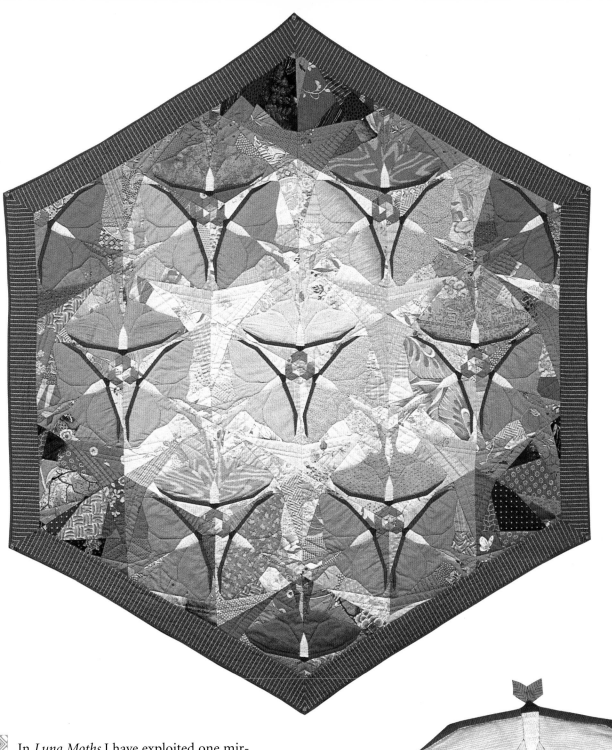

In *Luna Moths* I have exploited one mirror edge of the equilateral triangle block and P3M1 symmetry to make a block with half a luna moth.

Luna Moths
61" x 52", ©1982
machine pieced, hand quilted, cottons, blends, polyester batting (private collection)

Far right: detail of *Luna Moths*

P3M1

Above: *Bee Balm Screen*
64" x 117", ©1982
machine pieced, hand quilted,
cottons, blends, metallics,
polyester batting (private
collection)

Right: Bee Balm Screen block

Making Background Blocks

Bee Balm Screen was planned to explore
further the possibilities of the Bee Balm block
on page 21. In this quilt the square block was
used on point, combined with a much simplified version of the same block for the background and a new pieced leaf/stem block.
Using the stack cutting technique, and a great
variety of tan, yellow, and cream fabrics, I cut
enough pieces to sew all the background
blocks. As I sewed each, I drew colors randomly from the cut stacks.

Pinning the sewn blocks on the design

wall, I could then shift those forty-five
blocks around until the background pleased
me.

An alternative approach might have
been to try to decide exactly which one of all
of these similar fabrics should be used for
each piece of each of the forty-five blocks.
Realistically, the scale of the problem then
becomes overwhelming; the design requires
too many decisions; and the quilt is likely to
be left uncompleted. Chance is a great ally in
these kinds of circumstances. Some metallic
fabrics and brocades were used in the background of the flower blocks.

Left: *A Winter Landscape*
110½" × 68", ©1987
machine pieced, hand quilted, cottons, blends, silks, polyester batting (Southeast Psychiatric Hospital collection, Athens, Ohio)

Above: details of *A Winter Landscape*

Five different snowflakes, each from a different 30°-60°-90° triangle block, form the basis of *A Winter Landscape.* (See *Snow Crystals,* by W.A. Bentley for photos of hundreds of snowflakes). The overall piecing of the quilt was laid out at small scale on equilateral triangle graph paper. Fabrics came from many different sources, all cottons or silks. Many were used wrong side up in order to produce a frosty appearance. The grasses at the bottom are from a printed commercial drapery fabric.

P6MM

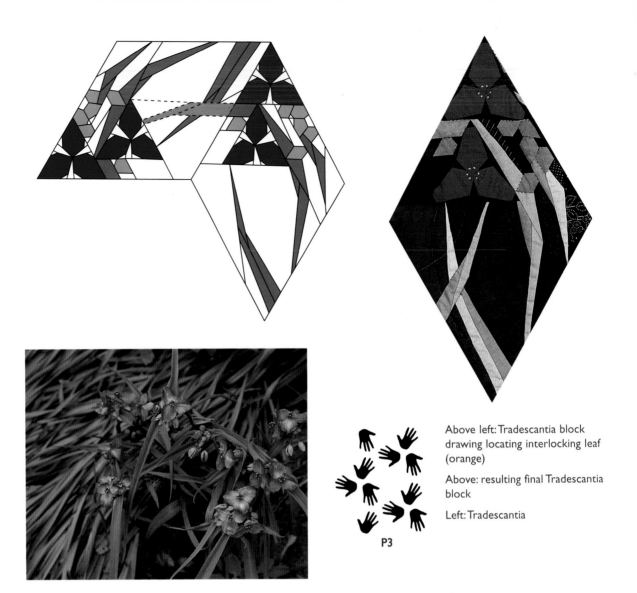

Above left: Tradescantia block drawing locating interlocking leaf (orange)

Above: resulting final Tradescantia block

Left: Tradescantia

P3

Spiderwort, *tradescantia*, is an American wildflower now frequently grown as a garden perennial. The three-petaled flowers suggest an equilateral triangle block. The tight bud clusters and the elegantly curved leaves are also defining characteristics. Working from a careful sketch of the flowering plant, I chose to fit two flowers, buds, and leaves within a baby block diamond (60°-120° rhombus) in an asymmetric arrangement.

After drawing the flowers, buds, and some of the leaves in the diamond shape, I made a copy of what I had drawn so far. I could then place one copy next to the other to see how the blocks lined up. Drawing half of a leaf on one edge of one copy, I could see

where to locate the other half on the edge of the next. Both partial leaves were then drawn in both copies of the block. In the construction, the quilt is sewn as baby block diamonds. When the diamonds are joined, the two portions of this leaf match up. Your eye follows the completed leaves rather than focusing on the underlying block edges.

Both *Aquatic Rabbits* on page 25 and *Tradescantia* (previous page) were designed by fitting the subject into a predetermined geometric block, unlike *Jack-in-the-Pulpit* on page 53, in which the block was designed to fit the subject.

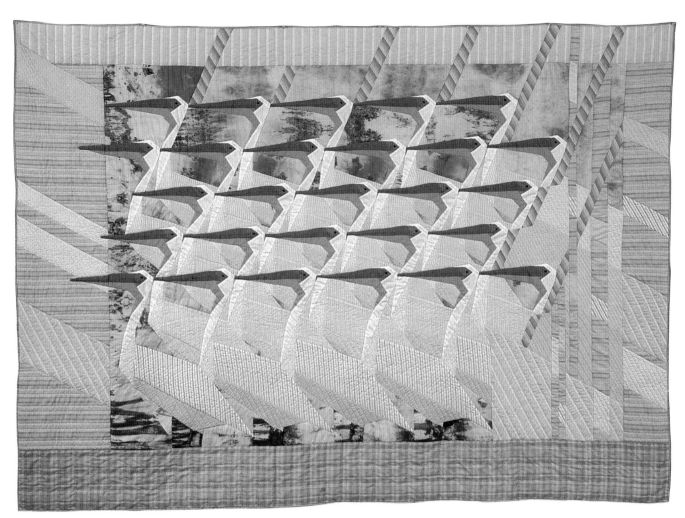

Another Way to Build Repeated Patterns

A slightly different approach to repeat design was used for *White Pelicans at Lake Edward*. For this quilt I sketched, then abstracted, the outline of a single pelican. After making multiple copies of the bird outline, I overlapped them, sliding them back and forth to arrive at a regular placing that appealed to me. The overlap then defined the repeat, and the array of heads in the center of the quilt were sewn from the resulting multiple-sided block.

A photograph in a bird book showed these amazing creatures, with blue beaks, coral eye patches, and yellow-orange pouches, all looking in the same direction. It seemed like a good subject for a block quilt. I was scheduled to teach at a symposium in California shortly after I finished the quilt, so I brought *White Pelicans at Lake Edward* along, thinking those California ladies would really like it. And they did, except they have brown, not white, pelicans out there.

Above: *White Pelicans at Lake Edward*
70" x 96", ©1984
machine pieced, hand quilted, cottons, blends, polyester batting (private collection)

Below: detail of *White Pelicans at Lake Edward*

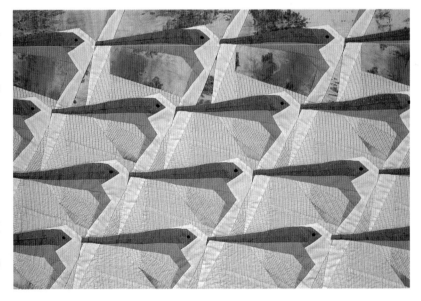

Selling my Quilts

Since I am working full-time as a quilt-maker to support my daughters and myself, I made the decision to sell all my work. Some quiltmakers find this a difficult choice. For me, it's no different than any other kind of artist selling their artwork. A few quilts I have sold the minute they were finished, and for those I never quite got the chance to enjoy them. For the most part, once a quilt is finished and has been hanging in my living room for a while, I'm on to another, and feel comfortable with passing the older quilt on to a good home.

Ultimately it's the process, and the learning, that are exciting. The individual quilts are really stopping points on the journey. There's a quote from Willa Cather's *Not Under Forty* I find applicable:

The artist spends a lifetime in pursuing the things that haunt him, in having his mind 'teased' by them to try to get these conceptions down on paper exactly as they are to him and not in conventional poses supposed to reveal their character; trying this method and that, as a painter tries different lightings and different attitudes with his subject to catch the one that presents it more suggestively than any other. And at the end of a lifetime he emerges with much that is more or less happy experimenting, and comparatively little that is the very flower of himself and his genius.

Plants in Pieced Blocks

As I continued to work with pieced blocks and with nature in quilts, several thoughts occurred to me. Very different designs appear, depending on the view selected, in approaching many subjects. A Siberian iris is a symmetrical three-part flower which easily fits into an equilateral triangle block.

The same flower from the side exhibits mirror symmetry, which can lead to a very different rectangular block. In both quilts, rather than piecing the very linear stems and leaves, I chose fabrics with linear designs. In *Siberian Iris II*, notice the brown grass on black fabrics used in the background; in *Red and Blue with Gray*, the vertical stripes.

Above: *Siberian Iris II*
61½" x 41", ©1984
machine pieced, machine quilted, cottons, blends, polyester batting (private collection)

Right: detail of Siberian Iris II block

The rectangular blocks of iris blossoms were made first, and pinned to the design wall in an arrangement that pleased me. The background area was then filled with rectangles and squares of various sizes to form the overall quilt top. This is one way to use repeated blocks to get some freedom to their placement.

Top: *Red and Blue with Gray*
39" x 73½", ©1987
machine pieced, machine and hand quilted, cottons, blends, polyester batting, ink (Brigham and Women's Hospital collection, Boston, Massachusetts)

Above: detail of *Red and Blue with Gray*

CM

In 1987, a good friend in Switzerland asked me if I could make a rhododendron quilt. Some plants lend themselves to piecing more easily than others. The formal structure of a rhododendron appeared to be a good subject for a repeated block.

Here, the sketch of a flower cluster was fit into an irregular block using mirror (CM) symmetry and staggered rows with smaller, simpler blocks making background rhododendron bushes.

Above: *Rhododendrons for Claudine*
44" x 39", ©1988
machine pieced, hand appliquéd, hand quilted, cottons, silks, linen, polyester batting
(private collection)

Left: detail of *Rhododendrons for Claudine*

With *Clematis Jackmanii*, I wanted a looser, airier feel. Beginning with a square block in which I placed a four-petal flower, two half-flowers and several leaves, I made several simpler blocks on tracing paper. In one of these I left the four-petal flower out of the design; in another, a half-flower; in a third, I included only the leaves. Setting all three blocks together with an underlying P4MG pattern produces a quilt which has both a regular repeat and a feeling of freedom.

Left: block details of *Clematis Jackmanii*

Below: *Clematis Jackmanii*
47" x 47", ©1986
machine pieced, hand quilted, cottons, blends, silks, polyester batting (private collection)

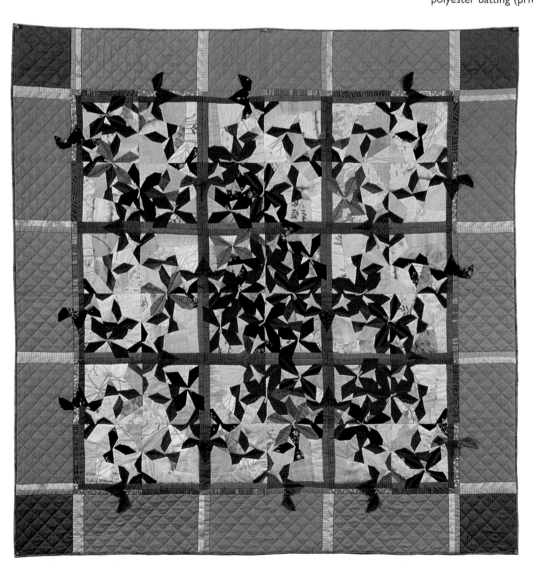

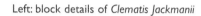

P4MG

My quilts have tended to become simpler, as I continue to work with natural images. It is a matter of how much you can leave out and still capture the essence you are after. In the first of the following quilts, the Lady's Slipper is fairly complete.

Lady's Slipper II
41" × 30½", ©1984
machine pieced, hand appliquéd, hand quilted, cottons, blends, polyester batting (private collection)

Right: detail of *Lady's Slipper II*

For *Dutchman's Breeches,* (a tiny wild-flower related to the Bleeding Heart), I've shifted the plant to a very large scale. I carefully pieced flower blocks and set them into a pattern of rectangles and squares.

There are no stems. The Dutchman's Breeches' leaves, which are very finely cut, have been reduced to a group of green rectangles of a patterned fabric, which work well to balance the flowers. The lacy patterns of the leaves are sketched in with a zigzag stitch in brown as part of the machine quilting.

Above: *Dutchman's Breeches*
88½" x 75½", ©1991
machine pieced, machine quilted, cottons, cotton batting (artist's collection)

Left: detail of *Dutchman's Breeches*

In planning a lobster quilt on graph paper the block lines were eliminated in favor of columns of piecing. One vertical strip of claws-and-legs alternates with another of feelers-and-bodies-and-tails.

Because of the strip construction, I was able to channel quilt this piece. What fun to go looking for raw-lobster-colored fabric! The flowery print on one lobster in the bottom row seemed a little improbable, until one of my students told me it looked just like a rare variety known as a "calico" lobster.

Above: *Homarus americanus*
76" x 54", ©1982
machine pieced, machine quilted, cottons, blends, polyester batting (private collection)

Right: detail of *Homarus americanus*

Solutions in the Third Dimension

Looking back, I realized I've found more than enough to work with as an artist in just the possibilities there are in pieced quilts. There are a few quilts in which the technical aspects of piecing have forced three-dimensional solutions to express the spirit I had in mind.

Quite often a flower center has rows of overlapping petals which make piecing extremely difficult. A hybrid delphinium has such a cluster of petals called a "bee" in the center, usually of a contrasting color.

Each flower of this *Delphinium* quilt is pieced within an irregular pentagonal block. The center "bee" is a small puff of silk inserted in the center of the piecing and tied down with heavy cotton thread "stamens."

Above: Delphinium block

Opposite page: *Delphinium*
67" x 60", ©1986
machine pieced, tied, hand quilted, cottons, silks, blends,
polyester batting (artist's collection)

Right: Mullein

Mullein is a plant of ancient uses, an escapee from Europe that punctuates the waste places here in New England. An eight-foot high candelabra, it makes quite a statement along the roadside, but is usually ignored because it is classified as a weed.

A biennial, mullein grows an enormous rosette of felty gray leaves in the first year. The second year it shoots up to six or eight feet, bursts into puffs of yellow flowers, sets seed, and dies. The dead stalks remain as sentinels poking through the winter snow.

In examining the characteristics that said "mullein" to me, I chose to focus on the candelabra shape, tightly clustered buds and seed pods, and puffs of yellow flowers. The leaves have been vastly simplified and the stem eliminated completely by placing a major seamline where the stem should be.

To maintain the puffs of the flowers, I opted for a three-dimensional approach. My flowers are made of two layers of different yellow fabrics ironed together with a fusible web. The web served to stiffen the fabric and allowed me to cut out five-petaled flowers without worrying about finishing the edges. The glue in the webbing prevented the edges from fraying. A point in the center of each five-petaled flower is gathered slightly and caught in a major seam. Similarly, the buds

and seeds are fabric inserts. This time, circles of fabric gathered around the edges and stuffed with a bit of batting are attached to the quilt by catching the raw edges in a seam. One half of each leaf is a faced flap, its raw edge caught in the seam at the mid-vein of the leaf; the other half of the leaf is pieced.

I wanted to quilt the piece by machine because I wanted the prominent crisp lines of machine quilting to complement the drapery fabrics used in the background. It is difficult to machine quilt a four-by-eight-foot quilt with three-dimensional insertions in one piece, so I chose to make this a quilt-as-you-go piece, using the seams of each candelabra to separate the sections. The quilt-as-you-go sections can be seen on the back, separated by hand appliquéd lines of black bias tape. Because of the way the piece was designed I could quilt each section separately, then join the quilted sections, inserting the flowers and buds/seeds. If I had used a different backing fabric for each quilt-as-you-go section, the construction process would have been more apparent.

To me, this is an extremely satisfying two-sided quilt. The back and the front were both determined by the growth pattern of the mullein.

Top left: *Mullein*,
89" x 54½" x 2", ©1985
machine pieced, machine quilted, insertions, two-sided,
cottons, blends, fusible web, polyester batting, cotton
bias tape (private collection)

Top right: quilt-as-you-go-sections of *Mullein*

Bottom: detail of *Mullein*

Above: back of *Mullein*

A three-dimensional solution was also critical to my *Blue Crabs* quilt. *Blue Crabs* started with a pieced block of the same kite-shape as the *Dragonflies* quilt on page 56. The center of the crab was placed on one long edge of the block. The crabs would be completed with a mirror block.

Atlantic Coast blue crabs are beautiful, with goldy-orange claws, blue legs, and greenish brown backs. I could plan how to piece the claws and legs (with a great many pieces). The body of the crab presented another problem.

The front edge of the crab shell is fringed with many sharp points. At the scale I was working, the points would have been almost impossible to piece. There is a part of the quilt world that gives you extra credit for masochism. However, there are even limits to the piecing that I am willing to do.

I considered tiny prairie points, rick rack, and a smooth edge to the shell. Finally,

I took two pieces of the brownish fabric that would form the shell, put them right sides together, and sewed a seam with tiny stitches that looked like a miniature zig-zag. After clipping and trimming the seam, I turned the body right side out, making a finished zig-zag edge. Then I slipped a piece of batting between the layers, machine quilted the pattern on the back of the body shells, and inserted these little quilted body "pockets" in a seamline that goes along the back edge of the shell and joins the leg section of the block to the claws. The crab shell "pockets" sit up on top of the legs and claws, just the way they do on real crabs.

Top: *Blue Crabs*
55" x 68½", ©1986
machine pieced, machine quilted, insertions, cottons, blends, silks, polyester batting (private collection)

Above: detail of *Blue Crabs*

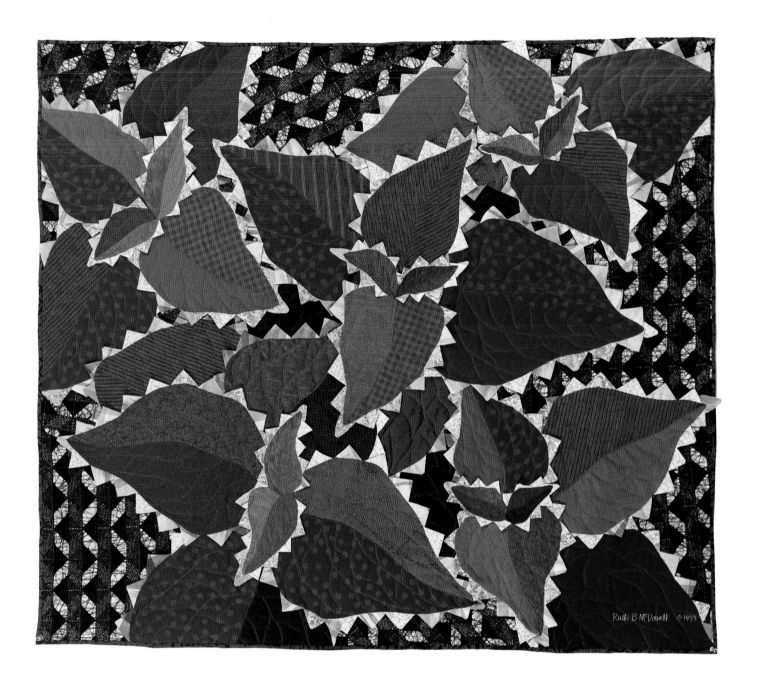

In discussing the translation of a coleus leaf to quiltmaking, I had often suggested to my students that they might be able to use prairie points, an old quiltmaking technique involving the insertion of triangles made from folded squares of cloth into a seam.

Coleus ellenhessi was made to illustrate that process and to commemorate the free spirit of a good quilting friend. The prairie points and leaves were cut first and pinned up on my design wall. The final fabric selected was the batik in the background. Its pattern of dark triangles makes visual echo of the light triangles of the prairie points.

The sewing process began with the pieces of the background. Along the edge of a background piece I basted a row of prairie points, then pinned the edge of the appropriate leaf on top of the prairie points, right sides together, and sewed the curved seam that joined the leaf to the background, catching the base of each prairie point in the seam. Working from the lower layers up, the last tiny leaves were finally appliquéd.

Coleus ellenhessi
43" x 49½", ©1993
machine pieced, hand appliquéd, machine quilted, cottons, blends, cotton batting (artist's collection)

Authority Figures

As you may have guessed from my description of The Twelve Princesses story, I have a significant problem with other people telling me what I can and cannot do. In the mid-eighties I got an entry blank in the mail for a major juried quilt show. It listed a number of rules for the entered pieces, then finished with the line, "We will not accept yo-yo, biscuit, or cathedral window quilts for this show." These three traditional ways of assembling "quilts" use different approaches to construction than the traditional top-batting-backing fabric sandwich.

Never in my wildest dreams had I ever had any intention of working in any one of these three techniques, but this was like a red flag to a bull. I made a small two-sided yo-yo quilt, *Still Life With Kiwi*, which I entered in the show, had accepted, and found hung in a very obscure corner.

Below left: *Still Life With Kiwi*
35" x 26½", ©1985
machine pieced, hand appliquéd, hand quilted, yo-yos, cottons, silks, linen, polyester batting
(artist's collection)

Below right: back of *Still Life With Kiwi*

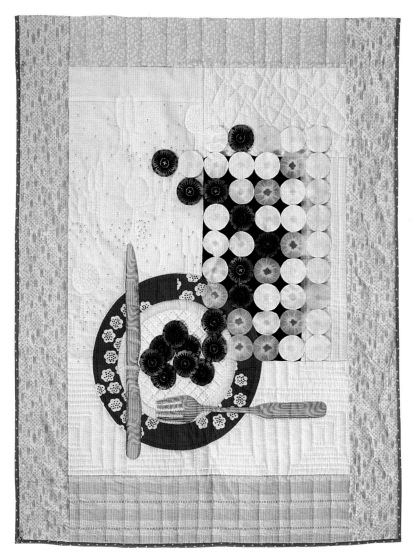

Above left: Indian Corn

Above right: ears of biscuit corn

Below: detail of *The Corn Goddess*

Opposite page: *The Corn Goddess*
73" x 92" x 3", ©1991
machine pieced, hand quilted, biscuit technique,
insertions, cottons, blends, polyester batting
(artist's collection)

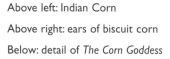 I also remembered a wonderful biscuit quilt, which I'd seen in *Quilters Newsletter Magazine* many years before, made of yellow and white gingham checked fabric. The yellow and white quilt had been rolled up and slipped inside a beautifully hand quilted green "corn husk" sleeping bag. I wish I could find the magazine to give the maker credit for such a wonderful idea.

The bunches of multicolored Indian corn displayed in the fall with pumpkins and squashes came immediately to mind. Using multicolored shirting plaids on the bias, I made rectangular biscuits and sewed them into two ears of corn. Time and inspiration ran out, so the ears remained rolled on the top shelf of my fabric stash for several years.

I would occasionally encounter them and wonder what to do. In 1991 I was working with a new group of batik overdyed Madras plaids, some Dutch wax indigo, and new hand dyed fabrics, and the ears of corn caught my eye. About a week later, I was quilting *The Corn Goddess*. It was great fun.

How this fits into my body of work, I haven't the slightest idea.

Cathedral windows occasionally reach the surface of my consciousness, but haven't yet materialized in cloth. There must be something I can do with them…

Ninety two inches from ear to ear, *The Corn Goddess* also includes some quilted, inserted dry "corn husk" flaps.

Above: *Brown Pelicans*
58½" × 73", ©1984
machine pieced, hand appliquéd,
hand and machine quilted,
reverse hand appliquéd, two-
sided, cottons, blends, polyester
batting (private collection)

Right: front detail of *Brown
Pelicans*

Far right: back of *Brown Pelicans*

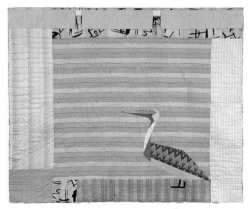

The *White Pelicans at Lake Edwards* quilt on page 63 was sold soon after my trip to California to a collector in Gloucester, Massachusetts, where there are no pelicans of any kind. This was around the time of the presidential political conventions of 1987. I began noticing certain similarities in the lock-step formation of the flock of pelicans and certain political parties.

Brown Pelicans is the result. The flock on the front of the quilt are all facing in one direction, similar to *White Pelicans at Lake Edward.* On the back of the quilt I appliquéd a single pelican going in the opposite direction.

Looking closely, you will see the flock of the majority outlined on the back by the quilting stitches moving in the opposite direction to this nonconformist.

If you look even more closely, you will see that I have snipped a hole in the backing fabric, removed a tiny piece of batting, then reverse appliquéd the eyes of the majority through to the back, where they glare out at this radical individual.

Landscapes

In 1986-7, feeling trapped in the grid of quilt blocks, I began a new method of construction by pinning a big piece of paper to my design wall. Taking a pencil, I drew a landscape of a pine forest. Laying a piece of gridded (eight to the inch) technical vellum, a heavy weight tracing paper, over the rough design, I traced the lines of the drawing onto the vellum with ink.

The ink lines would be seamlines in the new quilt. By gradually cutting up the vellum drawing I could use each piece of paper as a template from which to cut a single piece of fabric. Along any long or curved seams I draw a series of tic marks, which I mark in the seam allowance of the adjacent pieces, to enable me to pin them together properly when I begin to sew. These are equivalent to notches when setting in a sleeve.

Vellum is a heavyweight paper, with excellent transparency, that is available in architectural and engineering supply stores in sheets, pads, or rolls. It is not inexpensive. I use it because it comes in large sheets, is firm enough to trace around several times, is translucent so I can see what part of the fabric design will be included in each piece, and is available with a grid. The grid enables me to cut patterned fabrics precisely, vertical or horizontal, no matter what shape they are, and to square off designs and draw borders easily. It also allows me to combine pieced blocks with freehand drawings. If I am wise, I can take the final vellum drawing to a blueline (diazo) copy center and have an exact blueline copy made inexpensively, before I begin to cut up the vellum drawing.

On top of the vellum drawing, or blueline, pinned to the design wall, I pin roughly folded fabrics, auditioning them and beginning to make fabric choices. Cutting out the corresponding piece of vellum from the drawing, I put the fabric face down on the ironing board, the vellum face down on the fabric, and trace a pencil line around the edge of the vellum. I use whatever pencil I can see clearly on the fabric: colored, white, or silver if necessary. Then I transfer all the tic marks to the fabric seam allowances as well. I cut out the fabric piece with scissors, leaving a one-fourth-inch seam allowance outside the pencil line. Through practice I am able to do this by eye, without a mechanical aid. The pencil line on the back of each piece of fabric will be the sewing line. The tic marks on adjacent pieces will be pinned together so the seams match properly. All concave curved edges will be clipped as necessary for the piecing process.

Working on one section of the drawing at a time, I select fabrics, cut up the vellum, cut a piece of fabric for each vellum template, and pin the fabric pieces in place on the drawing on the design wall. Taping the vellum templates back together after I use them helps me keep track of the assembly process. When I have a large section cut from many fabrics, I sew those fabric pieces together and pin the section back on the wall.

Because I have taped the vellum drawing back together, I can find the appropriate paper template, if at a later point, I decide to change one of the fabrics I have chosen. In that case I remove the offending piece of fabric with a seam ripper, cut a new one using the vellum template, and sew the new piece of fabric back into the pieced top.

Other quiltmakers have other ways of working. Some use foundation or paper piecing. Some use freezer paper. Some don't use templates at all, but work with the actual fabric. Each of these methods of working has some strengths and some limitations.

Top: *Quiet Places, Other Paths*
68½" x 90½", ©1987
machine pieced, hand appliquéd, hand quilted,
cottons, blends, silks, polyester batting
(private collection)

Above: detail of *Quiet Places, Other Paths*

This vellum method was first used for the *Quiet Places, Other Paths* quilt. On a large piece of tracing paper I drew the trees, branches and ground. On a vellum overlay I began to consider how to incorporate the image I had into the medium of pieced fabric.

The trees naturally grow in verticals, while the ground forms mostly horizontal lines. I decided to work out the piecing as sections of ground and foliage between the trunks. Rather than adding a separate border, I drew a line for the outside of the quilt along the lines of the grid on the vellum, then drew another line four or six inches inside that edge. As I pieced my sections I changed fabrics at this inner line to form a loose border of lighter values.

Left: *Sumac Banners*
50" x 37", ©1988
machine pieced, hand appliquéd, hand quilted, cottons, blends, polyester batting (private collection)

Below: detail of *Sumac Banners*

One of the more difficult things to translate into fabric is the mottled light coming through a canopy of leaves. I found a solution here in the use of shirting plaids turned at angles.

Coming as I did from an engineering background, I first used plaids in my quilts only on grain. I admired Rhoda Cohen's quilts, with her plaids every which way, but I would go home and turn one of my plaid pieces slightly off the vertical and it always looked really dumb. Then in 1988 my plaids suddenly shifted. The secret is that you have to do this with conviction. Tentative gestures just do not make it.

Above: *Twin Birches at Long Pond*
33" x 48", ©1988
machine pieced, hand appliquéd, hand quilted, cottons, silks, polyester batting (private collection)

Above right: detail of *Twin Birches at Long Pond*

In the late fall and winter I often find myself looking at a distant landscape through a network of bare winter branches. In working out the drawing for *Twin Birches at Long Pond* I drew that pattern of twigs as a network of lines (seams) in the sky.

I had intended to couch down heavy thread along the seamlines after I had sewn the top together, but the quilt looked much better without that addition. That network of seams in the sky, emphasized by the subtle variation in the blues, makes the pattern of twigs for me.

In making a landscape of this kind, the most difficult part for me is to choose which piece of fabric goes where to capture the feeling of depth and the sense of light and dark.

Above: *The Yellow Maple*
68" x 86", ©1988
machine pieced, hand quilted, cottons, polyester batting (private collection)

Right: detail of *The Yellow Maple*

Hockomock
73" x 97", ©1991
machine pieced, machine quilted, cottons, cotton batting
(private collection)

In western Massachusetts on the Deerfield River, there are rocks with enormous potholes just below the Shelburne Falls dam. The rocks formed a salmon fishing falls a couple of centuries ago.

The Potholes at Shelburne Falls was made by working from a photograph. I was especially interested in the patterns of light on the water, the highlights and shadows, and the contrast between the water and the rocks.

Fabric selection started with a single fat quarter, hand dyed by Deborah Lunn years ago, in a netted pattern of grays, blues, and browns. Using that for the upper pool, and piecing it to use every scrap, there wasn't enough to finish the pool as drawn. A hunt through my fabric stash produced another fat quarter, this time a silk ikat of a brownish color, where the diamond-like ikat pattern was very similar in scale and feeling to the netting pattern in the hand dyed fabric. I pieced the ikat together with a scrap of hand dyed fabric to make the shadowed water at the back of the upper pool.

Water from the upper pool goes through a short fall, into a pothole, then into the pool in the foreground. I used a canvas weight upholstery fabric with a large design of cabbage roses in white, blue, and brown for most of this. A section of the right side of this fabric forms the start of the waterfall. The pothole and lower pool are the wrong side of the canvas fabric with a tiny scrap of the hand dyed fabric used as a reflection. In order to give the water in the lower pool some motion, and to disguise the cabbage roses, the canvas fabric was cut in several gentle horizontal curves and pieced back together.

The Potholes at Shelburne Falls
61½" x 25", ©1993
machine pieced, machine
quilted, cottons, silks, cotton
batting (artist's collection)

Ruth B McDowell
©1993

In building up a fabric collection to work with nature in quilts, you will discover that you choose fabric in a very different way than simply buying what's "pretty" in the fabric store. You'll need lots of off-shades of gray, brown, green, blue, and black, as well as mustard, purple, and rust. You may find you will begin to look at decorator fabrics to get some of the subtle colors.

My newest landscape began in the familiar way, with a full-size vellum drawing. I pieced the hardwood forest in the upper part of the drawing from many plaids at angles. Before I sewed the last two seams, which were planned to join the forest together to match the drawing, I talked the piece over with my critique group.

Rhoda Cohen took the three sections of pieced forest and, moving them out of a straight line, staggered them vertically. To me, they suddenly became much more interesting visually. I began to look at the irregular edges where I had planned to join the three pieces together, and at the cracks that formed between them.

It took several months to figure out how to carry out this plan. The sketched landscape was eventually made in six large pieces which were all shifted slightly with respect to each other. The cracks or spaces between the sections were filled with other fabrics, then the edges of the pieced sections were attached with a machine blanket stitch as soft-edge appliqués. The straight stitch part of the blanket stitch traces the original planned seamline. The perpendicular part of the stitch holds part of the seam allowance down on the surface of the underlying fabric cracks. Additional pieces of fabric were appliquéd to the surface of the quilt as needed to finish the composition.

I am very pleased with this piece and curious about where it will take me in my new work.

Middlesex Fells—Late Fall
65" x 90", ©1995
machine pieced, machine soft-edge appliquéd with a blanket stitch, machine quilted, cottons, cotton batting
(artist's collection)

Freehand

Having begun with the freehand drawing method of construction in *Quiet Places, Other Paths,* I began to play with the process. *The Light at the End of the Tunnel* started with an abstract pattern of arches.

Below: *The Light at the End of the Tunnel*
50" x 31", ©1988
machine pieced, hand quilted, cottons, polyester batting (artist's collection)

detail of *Poppies*

The fabrics for *Poppies* came from my shelves, multiple reds in cottons and a few silks for the petals, a green ikat stripe for the stems and sepals, and a variety of bluish prints for the background.

My introduction to the great range of cotton fabric prints and plaids came from Nancy Halpern's and Rhoda Cohen's work. Over the years Nancy, Rhoda, Sylvia Einstein, and I have challenged each other with fabrics. We all have very different eyes for fabrics, and naturally make different choices. If we see something that has possibilities, known or unknown, that strikes our fancies, we are likely to acquire a bit and share it.

Sometimes I encounter fabrics that make me wonder why they exist in this world. Who thought them up and what did they expect people to do with them? Sylvia came to our critique group one day with a five-yard flatfold ($1 per yard) that was an excellent cotton fabric, upon which was printed a sort of bluish tie-dyed sky overlaid by solid eggplant colored tire tracks and huge X's. She generously gave some to each of us. Rhoda used it first, cutting a narrow strip across the print, light-dark-light-dark. It looked great! By the time I had pieced two scarlet poppies three feet across, I could use big pieces of tire tracks.

You may also notice purple umbrellas in this piece. That's from Rhoda, a Dutch-wax indigo she found in Maine. I was startled when she gave me a piece, but it was very useful here. I focus on the wonderful irregular dark spaces between the umbrellas.

Gerberas, the colorful South African daisies, are large scale flowers with hefty stems. After working on drawing after drawing, I arrived at this very abstracted design.

Cut Flowers: Gerberas
70½" × 79½", ©1988
machine pieced, hand quilted, cottons, silks, polyester batting (artist's collection)

Top: *Freesias*
40½" x 55", ©1988
machine pieced, hand appliquéd, hand quilted, cottons, blends, silks, paint, polyester batting (Memorial Hall Library collection, Andover, Massachusetts)

Above: detail of *Freesias*

A flowering stem of freesias grows in a series of little scallops, each one holding up a bud. On the drawing for this quilt I focused on this pattern of growth, ignoring, for the moment, the flowers and continuing the motion set up by each scallop and bud in a line cutting up the background. This serves to integrate the background of the quilt with the growth pattern of the plant.

In assembling this quilt I pieced the stems, buds, and leaves with the background to form the quilt top. The flowers were then appliquéd by hand, inserting the base of each flower in a little gap I had left in each seam at the top of the bud. A little extra lavender acrylic paint helped make the blossoms stand out more from the background.

In Japanese tradition there's a white rabbit who lives on the moon, with a broom to keep it clean. At the Museum of Fine Arts in Boston is a netsuke of a moon rabbit. I included a harvest moon in the drawing of *aconitum carmichaelii*, a monkshood which blooms for us in October when the dogwood leaves are red, and adapted the moon rabbit as the quilting design.

Moon Rabbit and Monkshood
62" × 44", ©1991
machine pieced, machine quilted, cottons, cotton batting (artist's collection)

Lily of the Nile
65" x 51", ©1992
machine pieced, machine quilted, cottons, cotton
batting (private collection)

When there's a flower I love that isn't
hardy here in New England, I overcome my
frustrations by putting it in a quilt. *Lily of
the Nile* is a very much abstracted clump of
agapanthus.

So many flowers are soft pastels, it is sometimes a trick to keep them from looking too saccharine. By including a red and black plaid-like print on four of the *Bleeding Hearts* blossoms and throwing some bits of bright blue in with the warm browns of the background, I've cured that problem.

Bleeding Hearts is a good quilt to study to understand why I piece these rather than appliquéing. It would not be too difficult to appliqué this plant image onto a piece of fabric exactly as you see it here. What you would loose in the process is the chance to compose the background of many different fabrics. An appliquéd image tends to sit on top of the background fabric; by piecing the whole together I can integrate the background fabrics with the image fabrics in a unified surface.

Above: *Bleeding Hearts*
64" x 79", ©1992
machine pieced, machine quilted, cottons, cotton batting (artist's collection)

Below: detail of *Bleeding Hearts*

Cinnamon Fern
71" x 66", ©1994
machine pieced, hand
appliquéd, machine quilted,
cottons, cotton batting
(artist's collection)

As I progress, the initial drawing becomes just a skeleton upon which I hang the design. *Cinnamon Fern* started with a straightforward drawing. The first fabric I chose, to my great surprise, was a yellow and green batik from Africa. I had about a two-yard piece, which was slightly different in color on the two sides of the cloth. It seemed like a good idea to begin by making one entire fern plant out of the right and wrong sides of this fabric. By tipping the templates for the fernlets in different directions on the striped fabric, I could make the roughly striped design work for me.

Rummaging around on the shelf, I came across some dark Merimekkos® (hand screened cottons from Finland), which looked good behind the African fern. I needed another fabric for the second plant, and eventually found this very crisp ecru and black stripe. The remaining fabrics were chosen to make this color scheme work.

The resulting quilt is a long way from where I thought I was going in the beginning, but in working with this medium of pieced quilts designing often results in a dialogue with the piece in progress and the fabrics available.

Architecture

There are interesting connections between quiltmaking and the world of architecture. It probably has to do with a love of geometry and visual patterning. Nancy Halpern and Jeffrey Gutcheon both have architectural studies in their background.

The construction of quilts is very much like the process of building a building. Being involved in one craft makes you appreciate more of what goes into the other one.

My house in Winchester, Massachusetts, was built in 1840, and has a wonderful spiral staircase that goes all the way to the third floor, open in the center and only supported by the outside curved wall. Every time I go up or down the stairs, I give thanks to the carpenter who built it. It is an awesome thing to lay out and build and get all the angles and curves right.

A Flight of Stairs was inspired by a similar staircase at Gore Place (1810) in Waltham, Massachusetts, but this one has a diameter of about 30 feet.

A *Flight of Stairs*
47" × 35½", ©1988
machine pieced, hand appliquéd, hand quilted, cottons, blends, silks, polyester batting (private collection)

Uneasy Neighbors
72" × 66½", ©1987
machine pieced, hand
pieced, hand appliquéd, hand
reverse appliquéd, hand and
machine quilted, cottons,
silks, blends, polyester
batting (private collection)

The juxtaposition of H.H. Richardson's Trinity Church and I. M. Pei's John Hancock Tower in Copley Square in Boston causes a whole chain of reactions. It is visually a remarkable place to be.

This was a very unusual quilt for me, given the amount of hand appliqué it involved. Choosing patterned fabrics rather than solids for the church emphasizes the roughness, warmth, and detail of the stone work.

As a contrast, the Hancock Tower is made of Thai silk, cut so the lengthwise grain is vertical on one face of the tower, and the crosswise grain vertical on the other face. This Thai silk is woven with a lavender warp and a turquoise weft. It is iridescent. Since you are viewing the fabric in different directions, the two sides of the tower change color with respect to each other as you walk past the quilt.

Silk organza is laid on one face of the tower to make the reflection of the older building. It is held in place with the black lines of machine quilting.

On a much lighter note, I happened to be reading a book about Carpenter Gothic architecture while I was working on a quilt of fuschias in 1987. Here in New England fuschias are tender plants, usually grown in hanging baskets as summer annuals. The casualness of my watering habits in the summer means that fuschias do not do well for me, so I decided to make some permanent ones in fabric. It seemed to me that there were certain visual parallels in the shapes of the fuschias and Carpenter Gothic gingerbread. Since the pots of fuschias are often grown on porches, I made a fabric porch front that hangs about three inches in front of the fuschia quilt and casts shadows back onto the quilt and the wall on which the quilt is hung.

Above: *Carpenter Gothic with Fuschias*
98" x 91½" x 4", ©1987
machine pieced, machine quilted, cottons, blends, insertions, thread, beads, interfacing, wood and metal supports, polyester batting
(artist's collection)

Right: detail of *Carpenter Gothic with Fuschias*

Sycamore
74" x 52", ©1989
machine pieced, hand appliquéd, hand quilted, cottons,
blends, polyester batting (private collection)

The contrast between a prim little pseudo-colonial house built in the 1950s and a wonderful baroque sycamore tree of much greater age was the start of this *Sycamore* quilt.

The color gradation in the sky is made with the pieces of fabric between the branches of the pieced tree.

Above: *Leah's Tree*
37" x 47", ©1990
machine pieced, machine quilted, cottons, cotton batting (private collection)

Right: detail of *Leah's Tree*

Leah's Tree is one of my favorite quilts. The way the tree, house, and sky mesh is very exciting to me. Plaid fabrics are great fun to use in quilts. When placed with one of the grainlines vertical, they look like architecture. When placed off grain, they work well as landscape. Building a quilt of fabric pieces and making the fabric work as sky or hills or buildings is a fascinating process.

The arrival of winter focused my attention on the skeletons of trees. My sugar maple is clearly a sugar maple in winter because of the pattern and shape of the trunk and branches. By machine piecing this image I can design with the spaces *between* the branches, which is where the color changes in the quilt were made. The seam allowances of the pieced branches are pressed under the branches and then hand quilted in the ditch just outside these seams. This makes the tree image pop up and the background recede.

Tree Spirit: Acer saccharum
75" × 67", ©1989
machine pieced, machine appliquéd, hand quilted, silk organza leaves, cottons, silks, linens, blends, polyester batting (private collection)

California live oaks are very curly. In *Blue Tree* I wanted to appliqué the tree image so I had more freedom with the shape of the edges.

The tree is cut from a patchwork-like Merimekko print, hand appliquéd on a background of pieced Drunkard's Path blocks in three different sizes. The center 6-inch blocks form a 60-inch by 60-inch square. What are the factors of 60? Two 30-inch blocks, three

20-inch blocks, four 15-inch blocks, five 12-inch blocks, six 10-inch blocks, ten 6-inch blocks, twelve 5-inch blocks, twenty 3-inch blocks, thirty 2-inch blocks, sixty 1-inch blocks; or, in this case, fifteen 4-inch blocks make up the width of the upper border. The side borders are 8-inch blocks.

There are often parallels in the angles between the branches of a species of tree and the angles between the veins in a leaf.

Blue Tree
78½" × 75", ©1990
machine pieced, hand
appliquéd, machine quilted,
cottons, polyester batting
(artist's collection)

Tree Spirit: Northern Red Oak
105" x 68", ©1990
machine pieced, hand and
machine quilted, cottons,
polyester batting (Mary Ellen
Hopkins' collection)

For *Tree Spirit: Northern Red Oak*, a single leaf, greatly enlarged in scale, is pieced in the design of this quilt. Some of my tree quilts assume a magical quality; they become a spirit or essence rather than a real tree located in a real landscape. *Sycamore*, page 102 and *Leah's Tree*, page 103 seem real,

probably because of the setting and houses with which they are presented; and *Northern Red Oak* and *Tree Spirit: Acer saccharum*, page 106 are spirit trees.

Pin oaks are often planted in urban settings because they survive pollution very well. They are also very formal trees, with straight main trunks.

Using plaids as the background fabrics locates this pin oak as a city tree. The tree image is composed of indigo and white Dutch-wax cottons. A few pieces of dark and white plaids in the tree work to make it transparent; you can see the architecture behind the network of branches.

Above: *Plaids and Indigo: Pin Oak*
63" x 40", ©1990
machine pieced, hand and machine quilted, cottons, polyester batting (private collection)

Right: detail of *Plaids and Indigo: Pin Oak*

Left: *Copper Beech—April*
70" x 54", ©1991
machine pieced, hand appliquéd, machine quilted,
cottons, silks, cotton batting
(private collection)

Below: detail of *Copper Beech—April*

My hometown is blessed with dozens of huge copper beeches such as the one in *Copper Beech—April.* Their massive trunks with smooth gray bark look like elephant knees. In the early spring, the beech leaves are bright coppery orange. The ground under many of them is carpeted at the same time with electric blue *scilla siberica.*

As I worked on these images of trees I read more about traditional Tree of Life symbolism.

There is a quite remarkable consistency in the use and symbolic significance of the tree in almost all cultures and in the most ancient myths. Its original mythic function is as the center of the world, a living axis topping the summit of the world mountain and reaching up to heaven. The tree itself usually incorporates three levels: its roots grown down through the earth to the underworld, while its trunk rises through the world of men and holds the crown up towards the unattainable heights of heaven. In mythic tradition, however, it is not only the axis mundi, connecting the underworld with the realm of the gods; it is also the way by which the shaman ascends or descends on his estatic visits to the celestial spirits or the souls of the dead. And because it grows green again every year and produces the seeds of the future, it is also a major symbol of life, especially long life, of fertility, and of ripening and maturity. In its summer luxuriance and winter bareness it offers a symbol of life and death and of change generally. But the tree symbol is also tied up with the human soul and the mind, where it has to do with the unfolding of the personality and the process of spiritual individuation. A further aspect, exemplified by the tree of the knowledge of good and evil in Genesis, also occurs in Indian and Norse mythologies. This type of tree stands at the source of life and bears a fruit that grants enlightenment.

Myths, Alexander Eliot, ed.,
McGraw Hill, New York, 1976, p. 110

Yggdrasill
100" x 79½", ©1990
machine pieced, machine
quilted, cottons, polyester
batting (private collection)

The tales of the world tree are many. In Norse mythology the world tree is an ash tree called Yggdrasill.

In working with the image of an ancient ash tree I was reminded of some figures I had used in earlier quilts, images of women from a Paleolithic cave painting, "The Dancing Women of Kogul." The rock shelter in Spain in which this image appeared is very shallow, and the image has faded to the point that it can hardly be made out now. I wanted to give this first image I had seen of women in Paleolithic art a new life in my quilts.

With *Yggdrasill,* what was to be a small quilt changed in significance as I was working on it and needed to become significantly larger in size.

Whether the women are growing out of the tree, or the tree is growing out of them, I'm not certain. As I was choosing fabrics I began to use a streaky one with monkey-like or imp-like images in it. In the quilt they seemed to be protector images. The surface of the quilt is covered with many more protector imps I've drawn in with free-motion machine quilting.

Pattern on Pattern

So much has been done with traditional blocks, using them in new ways and new quilts, to honor their connections to the quiltmakers of earlier times.

At a symposium in Washington state in 1988 I was especially attracted to an antique blue and white Maple Leaf quilt, fairly roughly pieced and finished, but with a bold graphic pattern. On the long flight home I was flipping through *Tiling Patterns* by Grunbaum and Shephard, and came across an illustration on one page of a design made by overlapping different sizes of the same pattern.

 In this type of tiling, multiple layers at different scales of a single pattern form a complex surface. The *Maple Leaf* quilt came immediately to mind.

Maple Leaf is a Nine Patch block. On a drawing of a set of small blue Maple Leaves I superimposed a drawing of a set of red Maple Leaves. If the red leaves were the same size as nine of the blue leaves, many of the seam lines matched. This gave me a quilt easily pieced using three templates, and a chance to play with a red-purple-blue transparency color scheme.

Below: *Maple Leaf*
85½" x 85½", ©1989
machine pieced, machine quilted, cottons, blends, polyester batting (artist's collection)

Right: diagrams for *Maple Leaf*

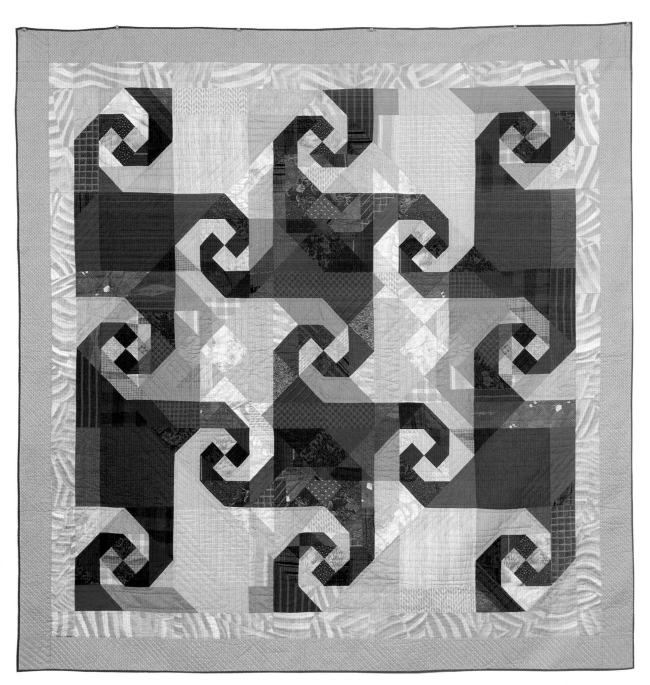

Above: *Monkey Wrench*
72" x 72", ©1989
machine pieced, hand quilted,
cottons, cotton/polyester
batting
(artist's collection)

Right: diagrams for *Monkey Wrench*

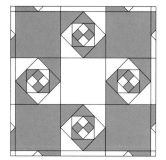

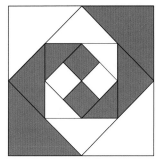

This first quilt lead, eventually, to twenty-one others, and my book *Pattern on Pattern*, The Quilt Digest Press, 1991. Many of the quilts were simple to piece; each explored a new facet of pattern-on-pattern designing.

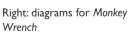 Two quilts were made of more complex overlaps. *Monkey Wrench* is designed from three layers of pattern: a gray and white layer, a larger blue and white layer, and a single red Monkey Wrench block.

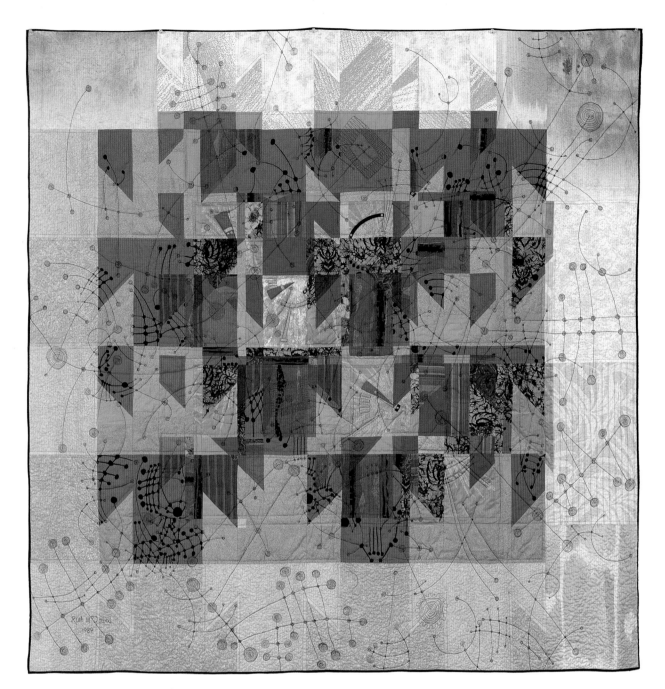

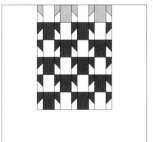 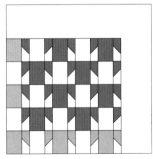 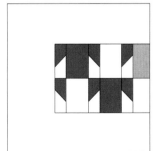

The multiple layers of *Double T* were drawn so that almost no seams coincided. A black design on one fabric was picked up and expanded to form the free-hand machine quilting.

Top: *Double T*
71" x 71", ©1989
machine pieced, machine quilted, cottons, paint, polyester batting (Brigham and Women's Hospital collection, Boston, Massachusetts)

Above: diagrams for *Double T*

Combining Freehand Drawings with Blocks

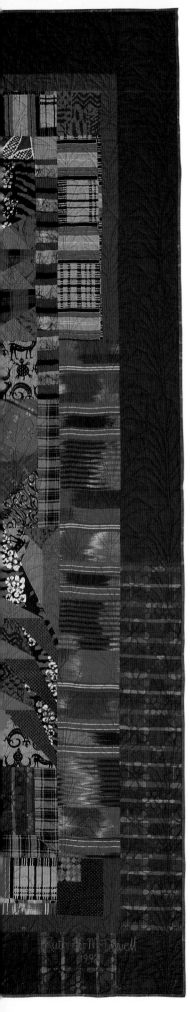

As I work with the patterns in quilts and the patterns in nature, I go back and forth in the way I view them. A series of more recent quilts contain both a freehand drawing and an abstracted pieced block of the same subject. One of my favorites is *Paintbrush*.

The Western Indian Paintbrush covers whole fields with color. The use of a simplified Paintbrush block with a detailed freehand Paintbrush contrasts the two styles of piecing I use and gives the impression of a mountain meadow in full bloom.

Left: *Paintbrush*
86" x 84", ©1992
machine pieced, machine quilted, cottons, cotton batting (private collection)

Below: detail of *Paintbrush*

☀ Two open blossoms dominate *Parrot Tulips.* Small side views of the tulips made almost traditional blocks in the background. There is a little yellow acrylic paint on the pieced blocks that I added to adjust the color.

Parrot Tulips
51" x 76", ©1993
machine pieced, machine quilted, paint, cottons, cotton batting (artist's collection)

Using the fabric collection I've acquired over the years is great fun. I especially love to use fabrics in ways their manufacturers never intended. Gazanias are amazingly colorful flowers, especially in their detailed centers.

In *Gazanias!* I've used nearly every polka dot I own, as well as a flower-power Merimekko rescued from oblivion by Sandra Donabed and shared with me by Sylvia Einstein. Fabrics from different years are distinctly different in style and color. Collecting fabrics over time gives the quiltmaker a chance to make much more individual statements.

Opposite page: *Gazanias!*
76" x 96", ©1992
machine pieced, machine quilted, cottons, cotton batting (artist's collection)

Left: detail of *Gazanias!*

Below: detail of *Gazanias!*

Magnolia soulangea strikes me as a rather Victorian shrub in its opulence. I've tried to express that in the choice of the fabrics I've used in *Magnolias*.

Left: *Magnolias*
58" x 84", ©1992
machine pieced, machine quilted, cottons, cotton batting (private collection)

After a wonderful two weeks of teaching in Fairbanks, Alaska, in 1991, I came home with a lot of new visual material to think about. The scale of the country up there is so expansive. I greatly enjoyed the quilters of Fairbanks, very independent women all, who took me to see things that were special to them. Several of them had an interest in weaving and connections with the use of musk ox wool, quiviet. Norma Mosso took me to the farm at the university so I could get acquainted with these animals. When I saw them, I had been very much aware that these ice-age beasts were looking back at me with

every bit as much intelligence as I was looking at them.

More than a year later, I made *Who Are We? Where Do We Come From? Where Are We Going?* Notice the ghostly pieced blocks of musk ox heads in the background.

Who Are We? Where Do We Come From? Where Are We Going?
45" x 73", ©1993
machine pieced, machine quilted, cottons, cotton batting (Cabin Fever Quilters Guild collection, Fairbanks, Alaska)

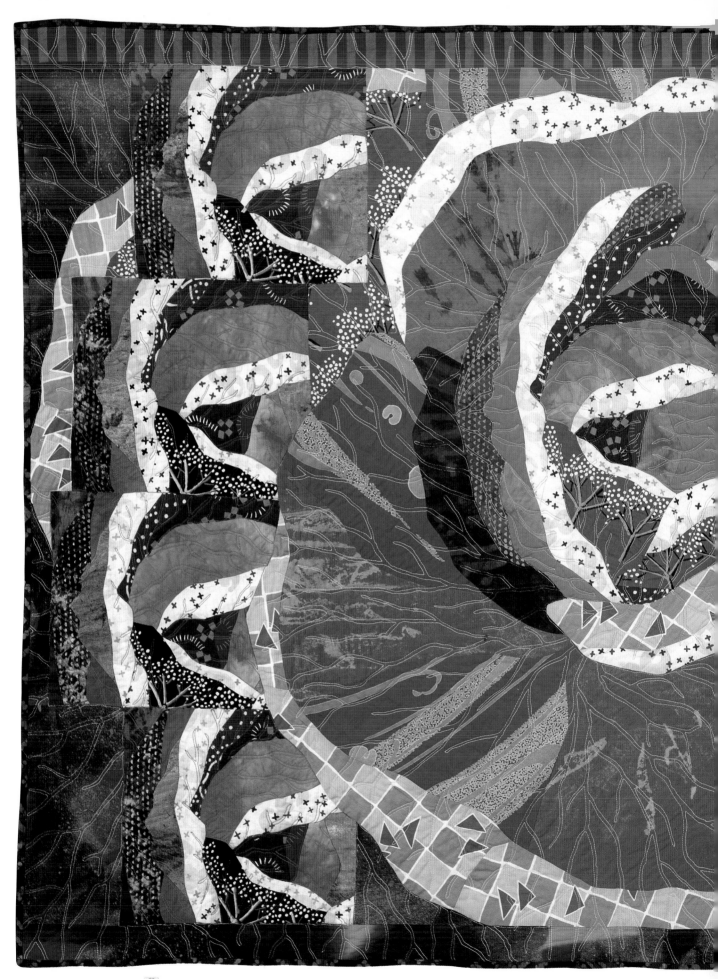

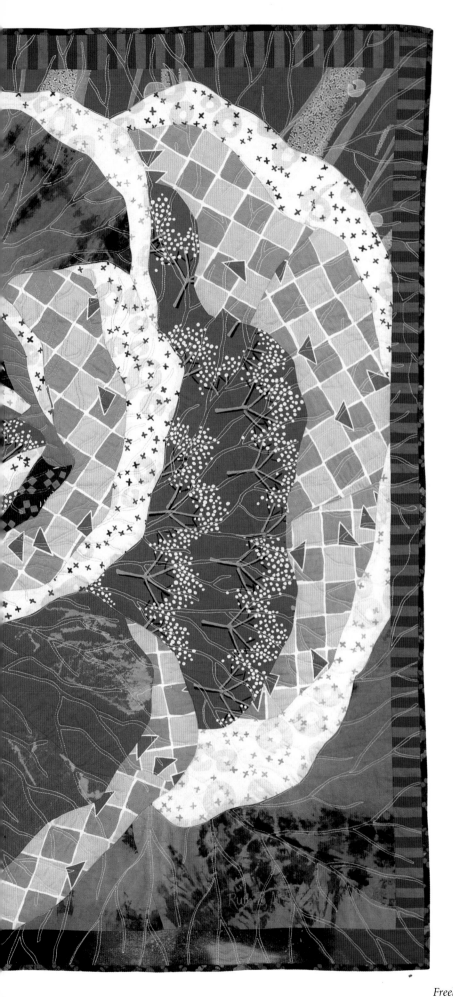

Alaska also has mammoth cabbages. *Cabbage* represents one, life size. Thanks to Jane Johns for awakening me to the possibilities of the vegetable kingdom for quilts.

Cabbage also contains many of the fabrics I designed for Kona Bay in 1992. In that collection I designed some fabrics with a variety of bits of bright white for highlights in quilts, a design element I found missing from most commercial quilt fabric.

Teaching is a learning experience for me as well as, I hope, my students. Getting a glimpse of the world through other pairs of eyes starts ideas which percolate through my brain and push me in new directions.

Cabbage
41" x 53", ©1993
machine pieced, machine quilted, cottons, cotton batting (private collection)

Trying to help students solve some of the problems they encounter in working with nature in the quilt medium makes me more conscious of details and visual parallels. In *Dianthus with Bear's Paws* I worked with details in petals and details in traditional quilts, looking for ways to connect one with the other.

A dianthus petal, with its zig-zag edge, reminded me of a traditional Bear Paw block. There are small Bear Paws scattered all over this quilt, almost like falling petals. In my quilts I delight in honoring the work of the quiltmakers who have gone before.

Dianthus with Bear's Paws
66½" x 92", ©1994
machine pieced, machine quilted, cottons, cotton batting (artist's collection)

People

I have tried to resolve how I want to express the people important to me in my quilts. I'm just at the beginning of that process.

My daughters have been such a part of my life that they have crept into my work most often. In *The Bathers* they are pieced in a repeat block, at the beach with sandcastles, when they were little.

The Bathers
32" × 70", ©1982
machine pieced, hand quilted, cottons, blends, polyester batting (artist's collection)

For *The Limb* I made them as appliqués, hanging off a tree limb with two of their friends.

Looking back over my work recently, I was struck by the branch in this quilt. I suspect it was the start of my tree of life series, considering the fascination I had with the pattern of the limb against the background.

Top: The Limb
36½" x 60", ©1988
machine pieced, hand appliquéd, hand quilted, cottons, blends, polyester batting (Memorial Hall Library collection, Andover, Massachusetts)

Left: detail of *The Limb*

"The Dancing Women of Kogul" described in the discussion of *Yggdrasill* on page 112 first made their appearance in my quilts in *Ancient Dancers*. They are appliquéd to pieced Penrose Kite and Dart blocks (see pages 40 and 41). Thin torn strips of plaids were roughly couched to the quilted surface as embellishment.

Top: *Ancient Dancers*
45½" x 78", ©1988
machine pieced, hand appliquéd, hand quilted, cottons, polyester batting (private collection)

Left: detail of *Ancient Dancers*

After the dancing women appeared in several quilts my daughters accused me of making single-sex quilts, so *Sylvan Pursuits* has both sexes.

Sylvan Pursuits
42" x 49", ©1991
machine pieced, machine appliquéd, machine quilted, cottons, polyester batting (private collection)

In feeling my way through this process I am beginning to get a clearer vision of where I want to go with figures. I want my work to be unabashedly quilts, not paintings worked in fabric. The combinations of separate fabrics forming images and a clear color statement are becoming my focus.

Morning Light
65" × 45", ©1991
machine pieced, hand appliquéd, machine quilted, cottons, antique patchwork squares, cotton batting
(private collection)

▨ Body poses and proportions are as unique in individuals as facial details.

Dressing Up
41½" x 50", ©1994
machine pieced, machine quilted, cottons, cotton batting (private collection)

Ruth B. McDowell 1994

I think the quilts with figures will gradually become simpler in some ways, letting the fabrics and the medium do the talking.

Sitting by the River Bank
38" x 52", ©1994
machine pieced, hand appliquéd, machine quilted, cottons, cotton batting (private collection)

Quilting Stitches

While I have been working through all of these quilts I have been simultaneously exploring the quilting process, that is, the stitching that joins the layers of pieced top, batting, and backing fabric.

Traditionally this has been done with a small, hand running stitch with cotton thread. The stitching often outlined the pieced design and/or filled in large areas with a grid or clamshell pattern. More elaborate quilting also included patterns of ropes, feathers, baskets, or other carefully drawn designs.

A surprising number of quilts from about 1860 on were machine quilted on home sewing machines. Many quilts, made for comfort, were tied.

As a beginning quilter I taught myself the hand quilting stitch, gradually mastering the techniques involved. My first quilts were quilted in traditional ways. As I worked longer in the medium, I began to think over the process and to experiment.

In about 1989 I did some extensive practicing at machine quilting in the pattern on pattern quilts with straight stitch, decorative machine stitches, and free-motion stitching, using a variety of threads.

I've become fascinated with the surfaces I can produce

with free-motion quilting, which is done using a regular sewing machine with the feed dogs dropped or with a feed dog cover plate, and a darning foot. The sewing machine does not control the length or direction of the stitches. That is done by the stitcher and is equivalent to writing a letter by moving the paper.

As I have worked through these quilts I have become interested in the patterns of the quilting lines themselves. If quilting is a hand process, why not take advantage of that? Instead of using elaborate systems of rulers, tape, compasses, and quilting templates to mark a rigid quilting design, why not learn to handle the quilting design freehand with as much facility as you would handle a pencil in sketching?

I have been investigating lines: those with smooth curves and angles, irregularly drawn ones, and networks of lines. The line left by a wave on the beach as it begins to recede made the quilting lines for *Blue Crabs* on page 75. Stitched with white cotton thread on the dark background, it adds a pattern of foam to the quilt surface. In *Cat Tales* on page 55 a line of curves and sharp points echoes the smooth curves and pointy ears of the cats.

Many overlapping snowflakes form the quilting pattern in *A Winter Landscape* on page 59, and many overlapping leaves in *Tree Spirit: Acer saccharum* on page 106. One huge maple leaf block is quilted over the whole top of *Maple Leaf* on page 113, from Pattern on Pattern. The traditional Noon Day Lily quilt block is machine quilted at the left side of *Fractal Lily* on page 46.

Many of the nature quilts use the sculpturing qualities of quilting stitches to add detail and three dimension, for instance, *Celandine* on page 18, *Poppies* on page 91, and *Aquatic Rabbits* on page 25. Quilting in the ditch along the edges of tree trunks or flower petals adds a three-dimensional quality to many nature quilts. *Quiet Places, Other Paths* on page 82, is hand quilted mostly in the ditch, as is *The Yellow Maple* on page 85. *Hockomock* on page 86, a very similar scene, has an overall free-motion pattern stitched across most of the surface.

In *Who Are We?* on pages 124-125 I drew freehand sketches of musk oxen on the back of the quilt and machine quilted those outlines from the back, that is, face down on the sewing machine.

As I work with free-motion overall patterns I have invented a variety of designs which I can stitch without previously marking them. *Swimmers* on page 15, *Baobab with Snail's Trail* on page 47, *Copper Beech—April* on page 110, and *Dressing Up* on page 135 show a variety of these patterns. The process of stitching these patterns is like patting your head, rubbing your tummy, and dancing on the head of a pin simultaneously. It's hardly the wonderful relaxation that many find in hand quilting.

The response to my machine quilted pieces has changed significantly over the last three years. At first it was, "What a nice quilt. Oh, it's machine quilted," spoken with a descending tone. Now it's, "What a nice quilt. Boy, look at the machine quilting. That's really hard," which is a relief to hear at last. I don't think a hand quilted quilt is inherently "better" or more valuable than a machine quilted or tied quilt. The total piece, the visual and tactile combination of quilting and stitching and fabrics, should work as a whole.

It is in the area of the quilting design that I think there is the most room for experimentation. Nobody is doing nearly as much as can be done. I look forward with excitement to see what the future brings.

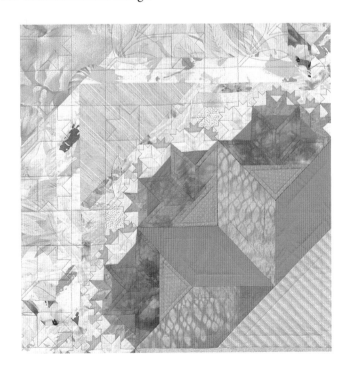

Free-motion Quilting Designs

Bleeding Hearts

Blue Crabs

Cat Tales

Copper Beach—April

"Damask"

Dressing Up

Dressing Up—Detail

Hockomock

Leah's Tree

"Loops"

"Torso"

"New Zealand"

Middlesex Fells—Late Fall

Conclusion

It has been fascinating watching this career unfold in front of me; ups and downs, series, and interruptions. I've skated on the edge of a lot of thin ice. I hope things will continue to challenge and change me, and that the process will never get too easy.

It's hard to realize now, that Emily and Leah are young women and on their way to independence. That certainly didn't seem possible ten or twelve years ago. Emily had ambitions at age seven for a lucrative career as a corporate lawyer. (When asked if she was going to grow up and make quilts like her mama, she replied, "No, because there isn't any money in it.") Both of my daughters have chosen to pursue their own visions in literary or visual arts. I'm very proud of them both.

Juggling the multiple roles of parent, breadwinner, laundress, cook, gardener, handywoman, chauffeur, and trying to work hard at this business of art has often seemed overwhelming. To be yanked back to a real-world crisis when I'm deeply involved in the design of a quilt can feel very disorienting.

It's a lot easier to buy nice fabrics than it is to make good quilts. Having to come out in the black at the end of the year, or to deal with a confined work space, are useful limits to work against. Think of what quilts were made in those sod houses in Kansas!

A few years ago the editor of a quilting magazine asked to come to my home to photograph my studio, as she had done of the studios of several well-known quiltmakers. I protested that I didn't think she understood the circumstances exactly. My studio is a second-floor bedroom of my 1840s house, fifteen feet by sixteen feet with a nine-foot ceiling. Sounds great, until you realize it has four large windows, three doors, and a fireplace. On the only large wall I have nailed two four foot by eight foot bulletin-board panels to the plaster. There are three bookcases three feet by six feet crammed with fabric, and piles of fabric on the floor and on the work table, which is rarely ever cleared long enough to allow me to work on it.

Assuring me that they liked to see the spaces as quilters actually work in them, and the quilt in progress, the editor and photographer appeared on a sunny day with their equipment and notebooks. After a few hours they had finished. When the article appeared in the magazine there was one small black-and-white photograph of me in my studio, and the other photos were of the outside of my house.

There have been plenty of times I've wished for different circumstances; for someone with whom to share the responsibilities and the rewards, or for some stability in the finances. I used to envy people who had a dependable paycheck at the end of each week, but in the current business climate, I'm glad to be my own boss. It has taken a lot of discipline to make this career work. At the same time, this is a lot of fun. Every once in a while a quilt will pop up just because it amuses me.

I think juggling the multiple roles helps me keep some perspective about what my ultimate goals are. The quilts aren't everything; they are just a visual expression of a rich and personal life.

I've had the opportunity to travel all over the world and meet and get to know people I would have never encountered in a more conventional life. Being able to help quiltmakers make the quilts that are important to them is the most rewarding part of my role as a teacher.

Having to find an answer to "Why?" has forced me to try to articulate in words what is happening visually in a quilt. Because of my lack of much formal training, I often reinvent the wheel as it were, rediscovering insights that have been part of the lexicon for centuries. This reinforces my feeling of humility. To be challenged to work with a student's collection of fabrics that is very different from what I would choose myself broadens my vision of the materials of quiltmaking. I've learned more from my students than they have learned from me.

I have used this book to express a lot of opinions, not because they are Right, but because they are mine. I recognize and celebrate that there are many other views of this quiltmaking business, as individual as the quiltmakers. As a community, let us celebrate the differences and delight in the diversity of the fabrics and the quilts and the quiltmakers themselves.

Conversation on the Porch
37½" x 54", ©1993
machine pieced, machine quilted, cottons, cotton batting (private collection)

Ruth B. McDowell

Index

Photo Credits:

Ruth B. McDowell:
Pages 17, 18, 19, 20, 21, 23, 29, 30, 31, 32, 35, 36, 37, 45, 54, 56, 60 left, 62 left, 67, 71, 73, 78 left, 80 lower right, 94, Personal photos courtesy of Ruth B. McDowell

David Caras:
Pages 15, 16, 24, 25, 33, 38, 39, 40, 41, 42, 43, 44, 45, 46, 47, 50, 51, 53, 54, 55, 57, 58, 59, 60 upper and lower right, 61, 62 right, 63, 65. 66, 68, 69, 70, 72, 74, 75, 76, 77, 78 upper and lower right, 79, 80 top and lower left, 82, 83, 84, 85, 86, 87, 88–89, 90, 91, 92, 93, 95, 96, 97, 98, 99, 100, 101, 102, 103, 104, 105, 106, 107, 108, 109, 110, 112, 113, 118-119, 120-121, 122-123, 124-125, 126-127, 128-129, 130, 131, 132, 133, 134, 135, 136-137, 142

Sharon Risedorph:
Pages 8, 9, 12, 26, 27, 28, 114, 115

Nancy Halpern:
Pages 21 lower right

Carina Woolrich:
Cover, 116-117

Other Fine Books from C&T Publishing:

An Amish Adventure: 2nd Edition, Roberta Horton
Anatomy of a Doll: The Fabric Sculptor's Handbook, Susanna Oroyan
Appliqué 12 Easy Ways! Elly Sienkiewicz
The Art of Silk Ribbon Embroidery, Judith Baker Montano
The Artful Ribbon, Candace Kling
Basic Seminole Patchwork, Cheryl Greider Bradkin
Beyond the Horizon: Small Landscape Appliqué, Valerie Hearder
A Colorful Book, Yvonne Porcella
Colors Changing Hue, Yvonne Porcella
Crazy Quilt Handbook, Judith Montano
Crazy Quilt Odyssey, Judith Montano
Crazy with Cotton, Diana Leone
Elegant Stitches: An Illustrated Stitch Guide & Source Book of Inspiration, Judith Baker Montano
Enduring Grace: Quilts from the Shelburne Museum Collection, Celia Y. Oliver
Everything Flowers: Quilts from the Garden, Jean and Valori Wells
The Fabric Makes the Quilt, Roberta Horton
Faces & Places: Images in Appliqué, Charlotte Warr Andersen
Fractured Landscape Quilts, Katie Pasquini Masopust

From Fiber to Fabric: The Essential Guide to Quiltmaking Textiles, Harriet Hargrave
Heirloom Machine Quilting, Third Edition, Harriet Hargrave
Imagery on Fabric, Second Edition, Jean Ray Laury
Impressionist Palette, Gai Perry
Impressionist Quilts, Gai Perry
Isometric Perspective: From Baby Blocks to Dimensional Design in Quilts, Katie Pasquini Masopust
Judith B. Montano: Art & Inspirations, Judith B. Montano
Kaleidoscopes & Quilts, Paula Nadelstern
The Magical Effects of Color, Joen Wolfrom
Mariner's Compass Quilts, New Directions, Judy Mathieson
Mastering Machine Appliqué, Harriet Hargrave
On the Surface: Thread Embellishment & Fabric Manipulation, Wendy Hill
Patchwork Persuasion: Fascinating Quilts from Traditional Designs, Joen Wolfrom
Plaids & Stripes: The Use of Directional Fabrics in Quilts, Roberta Horton
Quilts for Fabric Lovers, Alex Anderson
Quilts from the Civil War: Nine Projects, Historical Notes, Diary Entries, Barbara Brackman
Quilts, Quilts, and More Quilts! Diana McClun and Laura Nownes
Say It with Quilts, Diana McClun and Laura Nownes
Simply Stars: Quilts that Sparkle, Alex Anderson
Six Color World: Color, Cloth, Quilts & Wearables, Yvonne Porcella
Soft-Edge Piecing, Jinny Beyer
Stripes in Quilts, Mary Mashuta
Trapunto by Machine, Hari Walner
The Visual Dance: Creating Spectacular Quilts, Joen Wolfrom
Willowood: Further Adventures in Buttonhole Stitch Appliqué, Jean Wells

For more information write for a free catalog from:
C&T Publishing, Inc.
P.O. Box 1456
Lafayette, CA 94549
(800) 284-1114
http://www.ctpub.com